Railway Postcard Scenes

This book attempts to portray features of life involving railway activity or interest of one sort or another in Cheshire — as expressed through the medium of the commercial postcard. We have taken the liberty to define the county of Cheshire in the broadest, or largest, possible way, so as to embrace the old parts of Cheshire, such as Whaley Bridge which "left" Cheshire under the reorganisation of local government in the 1930's, and such as North Wirral, Stockport, and Woodhead, which "left" Cheshire in 1974, as well as new areas, such as Warrington and Widnes, which "joined" Cheshire in 1974.

A superb view, c1910, looking towards Widnes, of the Runcorn-Widnes bridge and the arches, beyond which can be seen the extensive sidings in the West Bank industrial estate. The writer of the postcard describes the view of "Widnes in all its glory". *Photograph: J M Ryan collection.*

It has been ou… Cheshire that in m… scenes at stations w… been altered out out of all recognition, the collieries, …, and docks that relied on the railway system for their very existence; railway architecture such as viaducts, houses, bridges, which reflected the individuality of the different railway companies and which were, and are, an important part of our industrial heritage; the construction activities of a railway system which permanently transformed the Cheshire landscape; and so on.

We have grouped this book very arbitrarily into four sections, based on Wirral, West Cheshire, Mid-Cheshire, and East Cheshire; we hope that this concept does not offend the purist who might have hoped for an arrangement of postcards on the pre-grouping lines. However, we hope that the postcards reproduced in this book will give as much pleasure to the reader as it has done to us to collect them.

We would like to express our appreciation to Cheshire Libraries who have agreed to publish this book; to the Ellesmere Port Boat Museum, the Halton Chemical Museum, the Nantwich Museum, Stockport Borough Libraries and the Warrington Borough Museum and Art Gallery, to V. R. Anderson, Heyday Publishing Company, the London and North Western Railway Society, and E. Talbot, in particular, for their approval to reproduce the postcards in their ownership; to M. D. Greville for his publication on the Chronology of the Railways of Lancashire and Cheshire; to D. Rendell and F. W. Shuttleworth for their photographic help; to R. Dean for the loan and reproduction of his Railway Clearing House Map; to K. Maddrell and the graphics and draughting staff for their work on the design and layout of the book; to Valerie Blackburn for the typing of the text.

We are anxious to extend our archival collection of railway postcards of Cheshire, and we would welcome the opportunity either to purchase or to copy postcards that are of interest. Don't throw away that old postcard — it may be more valuable than you think!

John Ryan
Irby

Basil Jeuda
Macclesfield
March 1987

A view of Wilmslow Station towards Manchester before it was rebuilt for the Styal line opening. There were then just two platforms and the place looks a little care-worn. Maybe this was deliberate policy if it was soon to be demolished. *Photograph: J M Ryan Collection*

Cheshire Libraries

91 Hoole Road, Chester CH2 3NG
ISBN 0 904532 22 4

Printed in England by Netherwood & Dalton Ltd.

The Railway Postcard

The history of the railway postcard is closely associated with that of the ordinary postcard itself.

Until January 1902, Post Office Regulations forbade any message being written other than on the face, together with the view or picture. This limited the attraction for communication.

On relaxation of the regulations, the postcard rapidly gained favour, as it had done years earlier on the Continent. Not only were cards SENT, as of now, but they were also KEPT to a large extent, being one of the Edwardian collecting crazes. We are deeply indebted for such behaviour, otherwise such books as ours would never have existed!

By 1907, some 800 MILLION cards had been posted in the U.K. for that year alone! Assuming a 'survival rate' of only 10% say, that still leaves us with millions of cards to find.

Just a very small proportion depicted railway scenes, amongst the vast number of greetings, comic, glamour and topographical cards produced. Of these, there were to be three main types:—

1. The Railway Official.
2. The big publishers' railway scenes.
3. The small publisher/private individual's contribution/'local' publisher.

In general, the 'interest' increases with descending order. The third type of cards are by far the most numerous in this book, and others of its kind.

A family photo taken in 1907 of Arthur Greg, killed at Ypres in the Great War, and terrier in one of the three hand-powered trucks on the 18-inch gauge miniature railways at Quarry Bank, Styal. The railway ran between the house and the weir. Note the small scale signals and the dumb buffers on the truck. *Photograph: B S Jeuda collection.*

THE RAILWAY OFFICIAL

Most of the larger railway companies had their own cards, being usually produced for them by one or more of the main card manufacturers. The London and North Western Railway, Cheshire Lines Committee, Midland Railway, Great Western Railway, Great Central Railway, London, Brighton and South Coast Railway and Great Northern Railway and many others figured here. The L.N.W.R. had cards of their trains, locomotives, stations, scenery on the line, road vehicles, shipping etc., and they sold widely. They were all of the Printed-type, though based, in the vast majority of cases, on photographs. Their Poster Cards, being coloured reproductions of their current adverts, are eagerly sought today. In contrast, a fair number of the Furness Railway cards were "real photographic", i.e. a normal photographic print of for example, their rolling stock or places on the line. Almost invariably, each railway had the Company Crest or Monogram on the cards — usually on the backs but not always (e.g., the L.N.W.R. issued quite a number with these on the face, on a 'light' part). The Midland had a series of Map Cards of their system, including Irish Shipping links using M.R. vessels. Again, these are cards of great beauty. The Cheshire Lines Committee issued a small series of cards of Cheshire Street scenes, etc. They are not easy to find.

In all, though, any work such as this would be hard to build-up from the total output of even all the 'Cheshire railway companies' combined, so wide-spread were the subjects depicted, in nature and location.

THE BIG PUBLISHERS

Here, we find a few major postcard companies issuing railway cards of their own right. Tucks had a series of 'Famous Expresses'. Wrench had a short series of, very surprisingly, the Mersey Railway (q.v.) but no others as far as is known. There were others, none of sufficient interest in compiling an area record. Incidentally, the Wrench cards are considered virtually as a Mersey Railway 'Official' issue by some collectors, though the Company device does NOT appear on them, nor any other special reference. The Locomotive Publishing Co. naturally concentrated on railways, and their numbered list of cards is a long one, locomotives and trains predominating. Quality, being real photographic, is excellent as a rule. The Real Photographic Co. of Southport had a similar output to their L.P.C. competitors, though probably less in quantity. They included ships, not usually railway-owned, as well . . .

THE SMALL, OR PRIVATE, OR LOCAL PUBLISHER

There are several 'names' of note, here. Warner Gothard of Barnsley concentrated on a kind of 'news service', in postcard-form covering disasters. He quickly went to the railway, mining, shipping, industrial or other disaster scenes, took photographs and information, afterwards building this into a multi-view (or montage) card with captions to each view. Much was usually made of the human element. These cards, too, are eagerly sought. The first railway one — as far as is known — was that of the Cudworth (Midland Railway) crash in 1909. This card was like a 'trial run' for Gothard, as it was very near to his Barnsley base!

Peateau of London produced fine views of railway scenes, mostly in the London area and of the Midland Railway. Again real photographic, they unfortunately tend to have faded, probably due to inadequate 'fixing' when printed. Nevertheless some fine cards are to be had. His total output will probably never be known.

R. Johnston & Sons of Newcastle and Gateshead in their "Monarch" series of over 20,000 cards, produced a number of railway ones, mostly stations but also of industrial railways and especially collieries. Messrs. Sankeys of Barrow had a similar approach. In both cases, the production of these fine views was 'local', but widespread within that area.

Wm. Hall of Widnes was a local photographer of merit, who also produced a little railway material, in a town which is now in Cheshire!

The private publisher is usually the best source of all. In many cases, cards were only on a limited 'run', and may well indeed have not been considered for sale at all, as all photographic printing paper of 'postcard size' seems to have been labelled as such until c1960. Almost invariably, the photographer is not identified, but the subject can be of great interest to the historian and general reader alike. We will choose one example — the interior view of Wilmslow station. This is so interesting because it shows the run-down station as it was before widening for the Styal Loop — the only example known to the authors. Who took it is not known.

Historical Introduction to Cheshire's Railways

Although tramways serving collieries and quarries existed in Cheshire in the 18th and early 19th centuries, the railway system first came to Cheshire as the Cromford and High Peak Railway, which was incorporated by Act of Parliament on 2 May 1825 with powers to construct a railway or tram road from the Cromford Canal, near Cromford in Derbyshire, to the Peak Forest Canal at Whaley Bridge; the section from Hurdlow (near Buxton) to Whaley Bridge opened on 6 July 1831. The London and North Western Railway leased the Railway from 25 March 1861, and absorbed it on 29 July 1864.

The Warrington and Newton Railway, incorporated by Act on 14 May 1829, was opened on 25 July 1831, and was absorbed by the Grand Junction Railway on 12 June 1835.

The next development was the St. Helens and Runcorn Gap Railway Act of 29 May 1830, and the section from St. Helens to Runcorn Gap (now known as Widnes) opened early in 1838. This Railway was amalgamated with the Sankey Brook Navigation as the St. Helens Canal and Railway on 21 July 1845; the section from Runcorn Gap to Garston opened on 1 July 1852, and to Warrington (White Cross) on 1 February 1853 and from there to Warrington (Arpley) on 1 May 1854. The section from Warrington to Garston was leased to the London and North Western Railway on 14 June 1860, and the St. Helens Canal and Railway was absorbed by the London and North Western Railway on 29 July 1864.

The Grand Junction Railway Act of 6 May 1833, led to the opening of the line from Birmingham to Warrington on 4 July 1837 with the section in Cheshire from two miles north of Madeley to the outskirts of Warrington. The Chester and Crewe Railway Act of 3 June 1837 led to the opening of the line from Chester to Crewe on 1 October 1840, though this railway company was absorbed earlier by the Grand Junction Railway on 1 July 1840.

The Manchester and Birmingham Railway Act of 30 June 1837 led to the opening of the section from Manchester (Travis Street) to Stockport on 4 June 1840, from Stockport to Sandbach on 10 May 1842, and Sandbach to Crewe on 10 August 1842. Another section from Cheadle to Poynton Collieries opened on 9 June 1845, with the section from Poynton to Macclesfield (Beech Road) opening on 24 November 1845. The Manchester to Birmingham Railway, with the Grand Junction Railway, and the London and Birmingham Railway, formed the London and North Western Railway on 16 July 1846.

The Manchester and Leeds Railway incorporated by Act on 4 July 1836, became the Lancashire and Yorkshire Railway on 23 July 1847. The section in Cheshire at Stalybridge was part of the line between Ashton and Stalybridge which opened on 5 October 1846. The junction at Stalybridge with the Manchester, Sheffield and Lincolnshire Railway was opened on 1 August 1849. The Lancashire and Yorkshire Railway was amalgamated with the London and North Western Railway on 1 January 1922, as part of the establishment of the London, Midland and Scottish Railway on 1 January 1923.

The Chester and Birkenhead Railway was authorised by Act on 12 July 1837. The line opened on 23 September 1840 from Chester to Birkenhead (Grange Lane) with an extension to Birkenhead (Monk's Ferry) which opened on 23 October 1844, and a further section from Grange Lane to Cathcart Street (Bridge End) opening for goods only on 5 April 1847. This railway amalgamated with the Birkenhead, Lancashire and Cheshire Junction Railway on 22 July 1847.

The railway linking Sheffield with Manchester was authorised by the Sheffield, Ashton-under-Lyne and Manchester Railway Act of 5 May 1837, and the sections in Cheshire from Guide Bridge to Godley opened on 17 November 1841, from Godley to Broadbottom on 10 December 1842, and, with part of Woodhead in Cheshire, the section from Woodhead to Dunford Bridge on 23 December 1845. On the same date a section was opened from Guide Bridge to Stalybridge. The Sheffield, Ashton-under-Lyne and Manchester Railway became the Manchester, Sheffield and Lincolnshire Railway on 1 January 1847, and the Great Central Railway on 1 August 1897, (which became part of the London and North Eastern Railway on 1 January 1923). The section from Hyde Junction to Hyde opened on 1 March 1858, from Hyde to Compstall on 5 August 1862, from Compstall to New Mills on 1 July 1865, from Godley to Woodley on 1 February 1866 (transferred to the Cheshire Lines Committee on 10 August 1866), from Hyde Junction to Marple on 1 February 1866 (transferred to the Sheffield and Midland Railway Companies Committee on 24 December 1869), and the section from Chester to Hawarden Bridge, 31 March 1890.

The Chester and Holyhead Railway Act of 4 July 1844 led to the opening of the section from Chester to Saltney Junction on 4 November 1846, followed by the section from Saltney Junction to Bangor on 1 May 1848 (only the first half mile in Cheshire), and a short section near Kinnerton from Saltney (Mold Junction) to Mold which opened on 14 August 1849. The Chester and Holyhead Railway absorbed by the London and North Western Railway on 1 August 1859, though the railway company was not finally dissolved until 21 July 1879.

The Shrewsbury, Oswestry, and Chester Junction Railway was incorporated by Act on 30 June 1845, and amalgamated with the North Wales Mineral Railway to become the Shrewsbury and Chester Railway on 28 August 1846. On 4 November 1846, the section from Saltney Junction to Ruabon was opened (only the first four miles being in Cheshire); on the same date the Saltney Quay goods branch opened. The Shrewsbury and Chester Railway was amalgamated with the Great Western Railway on 1 September 1854.

The Manchester South Junction and Altrincham Railway Act of 21 July 1845 led to the opening of the line from Manchester (Oxford Road) to Altrincham on 20 July 1849, the section in Cheshire starting at the River Mersey between Stretford and Sale. This line was jointly owned by the London and North Western Railway and the Manchester, Sheffield and Lincolnshire Railway. It continued to be jointly managed by their successor companies after grouping in 1923 until nationalisation on 1 January 1948.

The Birkenhead, Lancashire and Cheshire Junction Railway was incorporated by Act on 26 June 1846, and, was amalgamated with the Chester and Birkenhead Railway on 22 July 1847. The Chester West loop was opened on 1 August 1848, and the line from Chester to Warrington (Walton Junction) on 18 December 1850. The Railway became the Birkenhead Railway on 1 August 1859, and was absorbed jointly by the Great Western and London and North Western Railways on 20 November 1860; it continued to be managed jointly by their successor companies after grouping in 1923 until nationalisation. The line from Hooton to Helsby was opened on 1 July 1863, the Tranmere Pool Branch (goods only) in December 1863, from Hooton to Parkgate on 1 October 1866, the extension from Green Lane Junction to Birkenhead (Woodside) on 1 April 1878, from Parkgate to West Kirby on 19 April 1886, and the Rock Ferry connection with the Mersey Railway on 15 June 1891. The construction of the Manchester Ship Canal led to the Daresbury to Walton Deviation which opened on 9 July 1893, with the line from Acton Grange Junction to Walton New Junction opening on 16 July 1894.

The North Staffordshire Railway was incorporated under an Act also dated 26 June 1846. The line from Stoke to Crewe, and from Harecastle to Congleton, was opened on 9 October 1848, from Congleton to Macclesfield on 18 June 1849, from North Rode to Uttoxeter (to Bosley in Cheshire) on 13 July 1849, from Lawton Junction to Ettiley Heath, Sandbach, on 21 January 1852, and to Sandbach for goods only in December 1866 with the passenger service opening much later on 3 July 1893. The line from Stoke to Congleton Upper Junction, was opened for goods on 3 August 1859 (passenger service commenced on 1 June 1864), as was the line from Congleton Lower Junction to Brunswick Wharf. The line from Harecastle (Alsager Junction) to Keele was opened for goods on 24 July 1870 and for passengers on 28 June 1880. The North Staffordshire Railway was absorbed by the London, Midland and Scottish Railway on 1 July 1923.

After the formation of the London and North Western Railway on 16 July 1846, new lines were opened by this railway company from 1849 down to 1909, when the Wilmslow to

Levenshulme Railway (the "Styal Line") was the last new line to be built in Cheshire. The line from Macclesfield (Beech Road to Hibel Road) was opened in June or July 1849, from Stalybridge to Huddersfield on 1 August 1849, and from Crewe to Shrewsbury on 2 September 1858. The line from Winwick Junction to Golborne was opened on 1 August 1864, from Stockport to Northenden was opened on 1 August 1866, from Sandbach to Northwich on 11 November 1867 for goods (passenger service commenced on 1 July 1868), from Acton (Weaver Junction) to Ditton on 1 February 1869 for goods, and for passengers two months later. The Hartford Curve at Northwich was opened in March 1870, the Widnes Deviation line on 1 March 1870, from Waverton (Tattenhall Junction) to Whitchurch on 1 October 1872, from Runcorn (Halton Junction) to Frodsham Junction on 1 May 1873, the Over and Wharton branch on 1 June 1882, the line from Denton to Dukinfield on 2 October 1882 for goods, and for passengers on 1 November 1882, and the line from Davenport to Cheadle Village Junction on 1 December 1883 for goods and for passengers on 1 July 1884. The line from Stalybridge to Diggle loop opened on 1 December 1885 for goods and for passengers on 3 May 1886, the Moore to Walton Deviation and the Latchford Deviation, which provided clearances for the Manchester Ship Canal, on 9 July 1893, and the section from Dukinfield to Stalybridge was opened for goods on 1 August 1893 and for passengers on 7 August 1893. The Styal line was opened on 8 February 1909 for goods traffic and on 1 May 1909 for passenger traffic. The London and North Western Railway became part of the London, Midland and Scottish Railway on 1 January 1923.

The Warrington and Altrincham Junction Railway was incorporated by Act on 3 July 1851, and became the Warrington and Stockport Railway on 4 August 1853. The section from Warrington to Altrincham (Broadheath) was opened on 1 November 1853, and from Altrincham to Timperley on 1 May 1854. This railway was absorbed by the London and North Western Railway, jointly with the St Helens Canal and Railway, on 13 August 1859.

The Stockport, Disley and Whaley Bridge Railway was incorporated by Act on 31 July 1854, and opened on 9 June 1857, and the railway was absorbed by the London and North Western Railway on 16 November 1866.

The Cheshire Lines Committee was formed 1865 from the amalgamation of various railway lines, each of which previously had their own separate identities. The Stockport and Woodley Railway was incorporated by Act on 15 May 1860, the line from Stockport to Woodley opening on 12 January 1863. The Cheshire Midland Railway was incorporated by Act on 14 June 1860; the section from Altrincham to Knutsford opened on 12 May 1862, and from Knutsford to Northwich on 1 January 1863. The Stockport, Timperley and Altrincham Railway was incorporated by Act on 22 July 1861. The Chester and West Cheshire Junction Railway was incorporated by Act on 5 July 1865 and absorbed by the Cheshire Lines Committee on 10 August 1866.

Under the Cheshire Lines Committee, the section from Stockport to Altrincham (Deansgate Junction) was opened on 1 December 1863, from Baguley (Skelton Junction) to Broadheath on 1 February 1866, the Northwich Salt branches on 17 December 1867, from Northwich to Helsby on 1 September 1869 for goods traffic (the passenger service commenced on 22 June 1870), from Hartford to Winnington on 1 June 1870 for goods only, from Cuddlington to Winsford and Over on 1 June 1870 for goods and on 1 July 1870 for passengers (Skelton West Junction to Cressington Junction opened to passengers on 1 August 1873) from Mouldsworth to Chester on 2 November 1874 for goods and on 1 May 1875 for passengers, the Timperley Curve to the Manchester South Junction and Altrincham Railway on 1 December 1879, Hunt's Cross and Halewood to Walton-on-the-Hill and Aintree on 1 December 1879, the Warrington Avoiding line on 13 August 1883 for goods and on 7 September 1883 for passengers, and the Partington to Glazebrook Deviation — made to provide the necessary clearance over the Manchester Ship Canal — open for goods on 27 February 1893 and for passengers on 29 May 1893. The Cheshire Lines Committee maintained its separate existence through the grouping in 1923 until nationalisation in 1948.

After the Nantwich and Market Drayton Railway Act of 7 June 1861, the line from Nantwich to Market Drayton was opened on 20 October 1863. This railway was amalgamated with the Great Western Railway on 1 July 1897.

The Hoylake Railway was incorporated under Act of 28 July 1863, became the Hoylake and Birkenhead Rail and Tramway Co. on 18 July 1872, the Seacombe, Hoylake and Deeside Railway on 18 July 1881, and the Wirral Railway on 1 July 1891. The section from Birkenhead to Hoylake was opened on 2 July 1866, the section from Hoylake to West Kirby and the extension to the new Birkenhead Docks Station on 1 April 1878, the section from Birkenhead Docks to the Park and Wallasey branch on 2 January 1888, the section from Wallasey to New Brighton on 30 March 1888, and the Seacombe branch on 1 June 1895. The railway became part of the London, Midland and Scottish Railway on 1 July 1923.

The Macclesfield, Bollington, and Marple Railway was established by Act on 14 July 1864, and was vested in the Macclesfield Committee (in which the Manchester, Sheffield and Lincolnshire and North Staffordshire Railways were equal partners) on 25 May 1871. The line from Marple to Macclesfield was opened for passengers on 2 August 1869 and for goods on 1 March 1870; the extension to join the North Staffordshire Railway at Macclesfield was made for goods traffic on 3 April 1871, and the passenger service to Macclesfield Central Station started on 1 July 1873. The Middlewood Curve connecting this railway with the line from Stockport to Buxton was jointly promoted by the London and North Western and the North Staffordshire Railways and was opened on 26 May 1885. The railway continued to be managed by a Joint Committee of the successor companies until nationalisation.

The Mersey Pneumatic Railway was established by Act on 28 June 1866 and became the Mersey Railway on 31 July 1868. After a delay of many years the Mersey Railway tunnel was finished in 1885, and the line from Liverpool (James Street) to Birkenhead was opened on 1 February 1886, and the extension to Birkenhead Park opened on 2 February 1888; the Rock Ferry branch was opened on 15 June 1891. The Mersey Railway retained its separate identity until nationalisation.

The Sheffield and Midland Railway Companies Committee was incorporated by Act of Parliament on 24 June 1869. The Committee's line from Romiley to Bredbury Junction was opened for goods on 15 February 1875 and for passengers on 1 April 1875, from Romiley to Ashbury's for goods on 17 May 1875 and for passengers on 2 August 1875, and from Reddish Junction to Brinnington Junction on 2 August 1875. The line from Widnes East Junction to Widnes was opened for goods on 3 April 1877 and for passengers on 1 August 1879, and the line from Widnes to Hough Green for goods on 1 July 1879 and for passengers on 1 August 1879. The various lines continued to be managed by a Joint Committee of their successor companies until nationalisation.

The Midland Railway was incorporated by Act on 10 May 1844. It owned separately very few lines in Cheshire; from Heaton Mersey to Cornbrook (Manchester) opened on 1 January 1880, from Heaton Mersey to Cheadle Heath opened on 1 October 1901, and from Cheadle Heath to New Mills for goods on 4 May 1902 and for passengers on 1 July 1902. The Midland Railway became part of the London, Midland and Scottish Railway on 1 January 1923.

Certain powers of the Wirral Railway were transferred by Act on 12 August 1889 to the Manchester, Sheffield and Lincolnshire and the Wrexham, Mold and Connah's Quay Railways. These powers were vested in the Dee and Birkenhead Committee on 6 July 1895 and the North Wales and Liverpool Railway Committee on 7 August 1896. The line from Hawarden Bridge to Bidston was opened on 16 March 1896 for goods, and on 18 May 1896 for passengers. The Committee and Railway was absorbed by the Great Central Railway on 1 January 1905.

A view of Upton Station taken in August 1914. A view of the Seacombe-bound platform with the now closed signal box beyond. The station which opened on 18 May 1896 is now an unstaffed halt and this building has been demolished. *Photograph: B S Jeuda collection.*

Upton Station c1912 looking north towards Bidston and Seacombe. The main station buildings, including the booking office stood as an extension to the road over the bridge. These have now been demolished since the station was converted to a halt. By placing the booking office in such a position, passengers could purchase a ticket for either direction from one central point. *Photograph: J M Ryan collection.*

A view of the tunnel at Storeton Quarries c1912. This tunnel took the horse-worked Storeton tramroad (standard gauge) through a ridge of high ground in the Higher Bebington/Storeton areas. A steam loco. was used for a brief period. It was financed by Sir Thomas Stanley Massey, Stanley Bart of Storeton Estate and used former Liverpool and Manchester Railway fish-belled rail as specified by George Stephenson, noted railway designer-engineer. The tramroad opened on 15 August 1838 and took stone from the quarries to the Mersey near Port Sunlight and later the LNWR/GWR Joint Line from Chester to Birkenhead. The line closed in 1905 and lay derelict for many years. *Photograph: J M Ryan collection.*

Quarrying stone at Higher Bebington c1910. These large workings now filled in, were on the opposite side of the Higher Storeton road to the Storeton Quarries, and, despite being close to the Storeton Tramway, it never served these workings. However, there were railways here both for the steam crane up on the top level and short tracks for two portable steam boilers near the base of the workings. *Photograph: J M Ryan collection.*

Birkenhead's main terminus – Woodside Station c1910. From here, the Woodside ferry to Liverpool has operated since the Middle Ages, and the later steam ferry building is in the background. Woodside was an early example of a Transport Interchange, ferry – railway – tram and bus. The station opened on 31 March 1878 and closed on 5 November 1967. The main entrance had been planned to be on the south-east side, the tall arched entrance we see here was always the ''back door''. The parcels office on the left is now a public toilet. *Photograph: J M Ryan collection.*

Mersey Railway Loco No. 7 seen here at Rock Ferry was one of eight 0-6-4T locomotives built by Beyer, Peacock and Company in 1886 and 1887. Rock Ferry Station was the interchange station with the Birkenhead and Chester ''Joint Line''. This view is taken at the north end of the Mersey Railway's platforms, and the Joint lines are behind the engine. *Photograph: J M Ryan collection.*

Port Sunlight industrial village. This view c1906 shows the bridge near Christ Church and also part of the 2ft gauge railway used for transport of material from the works excavations to marshy ground adjacent in order to raise levels. This commenced in 1905 and the small locomotives were kept at work until 1914 when the filling in of Windy Bank Dell was completed. *Photograph: J M Ryan collection.*

A view of Spital Dam showing the railway to Bromborough Dock which Levers of Port Sunlight owned. Various private owner wagons can be seen. The significance of the horse is unknown. *Photograph: J M Ryan collection.*

Locomotive ''Lux'' owned by Lever Bros, of Port Sunlight, built by Andrew Barclay, no. 1117/10, was delivered new in November 1910. this locomotive was renamed ''Princess Mary'' in 1918, and the name plates put on an Avonside-built locomotive. She was sold after ceasing work on 13 March 1954 and scrapped locally. *Photograph: J M Ryan collection.*

A view of Bromborough Station c1907 towards Birkenhead. The station was located on the Chester to Birkenhead Railway which opened on 22 September 1840. The line was quadrupled in the 1880's by adding the Slow lines but is now down to two tracks again. A Down train – on the Down Fast line, is held by signal at danger. The station is now served by electric trains using the two nearest tracks and the waiting room on the left remains. *Photograph: J M Ryan collection.*

A motor train is seen here at Bromborough c1909 on the Up Fast line and is viewed towards Chester. These trains were cheaper to run than the more orthodox locomotive and coaches and were akin to the present diesel multiple units. The footbridge will be familiar to present users of the station. *Photograph: J M Ryan collection.*

A view of Hooton Station c1912 towards Woodside, Birkenhead. The station opened on 22 September 1840 and became a junction for the branches to Helsby and West Kirby. The main station buildings in the background are on the Up (east) side and seem a little inadequate in relation to the size of the place. The freight train is on the Up Fast line which is now the site of a run-round loop. *Photograph: J M Ryan collection.*

Hadlow Road Station is viewed towards Hooton c1905. A freight train is just entering the loop. The station closed to passenger traffic on 17 September 1956 and completely on withdrawal of the freight traffic on 7 May 1962. However, unlike other stations on the branch, it was not demolished and is now preserved as a "typical country station", being part of the Wirral Way Country Park. *Photograph: E Talbot collection.*

Neston Station, c1904 viewed towards Hooton and a short Hooton-West Kirby train has arrived. The station opened on 1 October 1866, closed to passengers on 17 September 1956 and entirely on 7 May 1962. No loop was ever provided here, unlike at Hadlow Road Station and it remained single platformed. Neston was an important south Wirral town, reflected in the provision of a much more substantial building than at Hadlow Road – or, indeed any other station bar Heswall. Note the agricultural implements. The railway carried anything in those days! *Photograph: J M Ryan collection.*

A view of Heswall Station c1915 with a Hooton to West Kirby train calling with plenty of potential passengers. A Great Western engine is hauling LNWR stock, a common sight on this joint line. The single-line staff is held by the rail man next to the engine and would be for either the section from Parkgate to Heswall or Heswall to Thurstaston. *Photograph: J M Ryan collection.*

Heswall Station c1900 viewed towards West Kirby as a train for Neston (and beyond) enters. Note the small signal box on the platform, to an LNWR design, and the tall station house by the footbridge steps. *Photograph: B S Jeuda collection.*

A view of Little Sutton Station looking towards Helsby. Note the substantial sandstone buildings of pleasing architecture. Save for the addition of a footbridge at the Hooton end, the scene is not greatly changed. *Photograph: Heyday Publishing Company.*

Ellesmere Port. A view of the New Mills c1910 showing the grain elevator and coal tip. The town grew up as a transport interchange on opening of the Ellesmere – later Shropshire Union Canal. Later came railways and the Manchester Ship Canal. 'Some Industries' also grew and a few floundered there. The coal interchange is overshadowed by the new mills. Pearson and Knowles were a large Lancashire coal mine owner and coal factors. *Photograph: Ellesmere Port Boat Museum.*

Another view of the New Mills and Docks at Ellesmere Port. Ellesmere Port is still a busy port and this view shows the interchange facilities between rail and water. Note the wagon turntable for getting round right-angle bends. The barges are suitable for both the Mersey and Weaver Navigation as well as the later Manchester Ship Canal. The flour mills were developed here bearing in mind the excellent transport links. *Photograph: Ellesmere Port Boat Museum.*

A view of Ellesmere Port Station c1905 looking towards Hooton. A local train enters past the level crossing with a good number of potential passengers. The old locomotive shed is beyond the crossing – it was later owned by the Manchester Ship Canal Co and used for their engines. The level crossing is now closed and replaced by an overbridge, and there is also a footbridge. The station opened with the line on 1 July 1863, named Whitby Locks, and renamed Ellesmere Port in 1870. Note architectural features which are the same as Little Sutton. *Photograph: LNWR Society.*

The Mersey Tunnel Tower, Birkenhead c1904, was one of the ''Several Wonders of Birkenhead''. This edifice still dominates Hamilton Square Station. In those days the ''Mersey Tunnel'' was the Railway, not the road, as the present motor-orientated public think. The title is not quite accurate – the tower was provided to supply water under pressure to power the large public lifts from the upper to the lower level of the station. When the lifts were altered and electrified, firstly during the 1930's, the Mersey Railway Co retained the tower – possible because of the extreme difficulty in demolishing it! Note the then, new, Birkenhead Corporation Tram Car no. 55. A similar car no. 20 has been preserved. *Photograph: J M Ryan collection.*

The Booking Hall at Hamilton Square Station showing the original booking office in the Booking Hall still familiar to today's travellers. The entrances to the big hydraulic lifts can be seen left, and (right) between the short railings. *Photograph: E Talbot collection.*

This photograph of Birkenhead Central Station c1905 shows Birkenhead Central after the electrification which was completed in May 1903. This was to re-generate completely the financial fortunes of the railway. Note the mechanical signalling then in use, and the fourth or negative rail between the running rails, which has now been removed. The traction depot is on the right, developed from the old steam shed which served the whole of the original Mersey Railway. *Photograph: E Talbot collection.*

The exterior of Birkenhead Central Station is part of a fine street scene of the 1920's with vintage motors, private and commercial. At this time, trams still ran in Birkenhead but the Corporation was an early operator of petrol buses – maybe taking its cue from the Mersey Railway's own initial operation of such vehicles. BCT no. 22 trundles through a scene which is now unrecognisable due to the flyover of the Mersey Road Tunnel approach. Happily, the curved awning remains, but potential bus users can no longer shelter under it due to the stop relocation – again due to that flyover. *Photograph: Heyday Publishing Company.*

A photograph of Loco no. 6 at Birkenhead Central. This is one of the powerful 0-6-4T locos built by Beyer Peacock of Gorton in 1886/87. Fox was named after an Engineer. The large pipe running from near the front of the loco back to the tank top took exhaust steam from one cylinder and condensed it, this being done to cut down the amount of steam vapour released into the tunnel sections. There was an identical pipe on the other side of the loco. The system worked, and allowed the engine to run further between water stops as well, but the exhaust still made the tunnels and tunnel stations very unpleasant, leading to large traffic losses as people deserted for the fresh air of the ferries. *Photograph: J M Ryan collection.*

Park Station, Duke Street, Birkenhead c1908. "Park Joint Station shortest and quickest route to Liverpool, Hoylake, West Kirby, Wallasey and New Brighton" reads the prominent fascia sign. This was and indeed still is true. The reference to "Joint" is interesting – the station was jointly operated by the Mersey and Wirral Companies, both lines' trains terminating here. For many years, the former was electrified, and though electric running came only in March 1938 when the L.M.S.R. provided new stock, (only recently withdrawn) on the initiation of their Wirral electrification. *Photograph: J M Ryan collection*

This photograph is of the Electric Coal Conveyor at Birkenhead. This is a Mersey Docks and Harbour Board promotional card of the 1930's and indicates the extent of local shipments in those days. The 'private owner' wagons of some eight different coal factors or collieries are to be seen from such areas as Lancashire, North Staffordshire and North Wales. The ship is taking on 'bunker coal' for her own boilers. *Photograph: J M Ryan collection.*

Seacombe Station c1908 shows a busy scene at this Wirral Railway terminus, built and opened on 1 June 1895 by the Wirral Railway. The station closed to passengers on 4 January 1960. This place always had the appearance of being "temporary". The Wrexham service of the Great Central Railway ran from here.
Photograph: Heyday Publishing Company.

Liscard & Poulton. A humorous card of this little-known Wirral Railway Station on the branch to Seacombe. The station opened on 1 June 1895 and closed to passengers in January 1960 and to all traffic on 5 December 1960. It is now 'lost' in the widened rock cutting for the second Mersey Road Tunnel approach road. In any case, it was of simple timber building construction on a single island platform. *Photograph: J M Ryan collection*

A photograph of 2-4-OT No. 3 c1910, probably at Slopes Branch Junction where the Birkenhead Slopes Branch (to the docks) left the line from Seacombe Junction to Seacombe. It was built by Beyer Peacock in 1884 for the Seacombe Hoylake and Deeside Railway. The coal rails were added later to increase coal capacity of the tiny bunker from 1½ tons to 2 tons. No. 3 was withdrawn from service in February 1914. *Photograph: J M Ryan collection.*

An exterior view of New Brighton Station c1910. Except for the large sign, some people must have missed the station from time to time. The scene has changed very litte. *Photograph: Heyday Publishing Company.*

New Brighton Station viewed towards Seacombe Junction. The small goods and coal yard is to the right whilst a large 4-4-2T or 4-4-4T has arrived with an eight coach train. Electrification was inaugerated on 13 March 1938. The goods yard and depot closed on 30 November 1965. The Hotel Victoria is still a notable feature above the station, today. *Photograph: J M Ryan collection.*

A photograph of locomotive No. 12 on a New Brighton-Birkenhead North train. It was one of two No. 0-6-4T locomotives built in 1900 by Beyer, Peacock and Company. They saw little use in passenger traffic, and No.12 was withdrawn in February 1924. The railway was and still is inundated by wind blown sand along here as was Warren Station which was closed to all traffic on 1 October 1915 and of which there is now no trace. The train is seen here running from New Brighton and the sea can be glimpsed (left). *Photograph: J M Ryan collection.*

A view of Wallasey Station c1910 towards New Brighton. The station opened 2 January 1888 and was a terminus until the line extended to New Brighton (30.3.1888). Loco. No. 5, hauling the Birkenhead Park bound train, was built by Beyer Peacock in August 1887 as loco No. 7 (it was renumbered in 1895). The main station building is little altered to date and the same applies to the footbridge. This station is now named Wallasey Grove Road, to distinguish it from the more recent Wallasey Village Station. *Photograph J M Ryan collection.*

Wallasey Station seen here from the sand hills c1905 is visible in the centre background. This view emphasises the surroundings of the typical suburban station in the Edwardian period. *Photograph J M Ryan collection.*

Leasowe Station viewed towards Birkenhead c1905. The station was rebuilt in June 1894 for the track doubling of the Bidston to Hoylake section. The small timber shed was the original signal box. It did not control the gates, which were swung by hand. Note the mid-Victorian home signal with lamp and spectacle casing part way down the post. *Photograph J M Ryan collection.*

Moreton Station c1905 viewed east. Note the simple signal box (closed 1951 and replaced by a larger one) on the West Kirby bound platform. Moreton was then just a village, and the simple station reflects that fact. A small goods and coal yard, closed 1965, lay behind the small signal box. *Photograph J M Ryan collection.*

The station at Moreton viewed north-east from Moreton Road, c1930. A great change has occurred compared with the other photograph. Moreton is expanding both in variety, style and appearance. An LNWR engine is in charge of a West Kirby train. Such was the increase in traffic, that by the end of the decade, the LMS had electrified the line and rebuilt the station. Cadbury's Chocolate Factory now sits on the site of these 'pre fabs'. *Photograph J M Ryan collection.*

Meols Station 1910 viewed north. Except for the train and station building, not a lot has changed here. The lake is still very prominent, so preventing the close approach of housing on the south side. *Photograph: J M Ryan collection.*

The Railway Cottage at Meols c1908. A Birkenhead Park bound train hurries past this pleasant building of a style very close to that of Leasowe. The train is a typical Wirral Railway one of the period. Note the width across the guards compartment with his view onto the track like one of the cabs of present day trains. This is a flat area, largely undeveloped even today, between Meols and Hoylake and the level crossing still exists. *Photograph: J M Ryan collection.*

A view taken of Hoylake Station c1906 in the north-western direction – probably from a gasholder of Hoylake Gasworks. The long, narrow, timber building on the left hand side was the Wirral Railway Carriage Works and Paint Shop, closed in the 1920's. Note the busy-looking coal yard to the north of the main line. It was closed in 1965. *Photograph: J M Ryan collection.*

The second view of Hoylake Station is east towards Birkenhead. The West Kirby bound train is hauled by loco No. 11. Designed by Mr Baker and built in 1896, it was Britain's very first 4-4-4T. Manufactured by Beyer Peacock and Co of Gorton, it was taken out of passenger service in 1919 and scrapped in February 1920. Note the mixed architectural styles of station building and the all-pervading gas works. *Photograph: J M Ryan collection.*

A view of West Kirby Station taken from the road bridge c1908 and looking south. Here was the junction in later years with the LNWR/GWR joint line from Neston, and the joint line station was to the left and out of the picture. The large goods depot in the centre of the scene was the site of the original station built by the Seacombe, Hoylake and Deeside Railway and which was closed in 1896. Taking water in the centre of the photograph, is Wirral Railway 0-4-4T No. 7 at the head of a passenger train for Birkenhead Park. *Photograph: J M Ryan collection.*

This was the Wirral Railway's only locomotive depot. It was not a works as such, major overhauls being carried out by Messrs Beyer Peacock at Gorton, and other smaller jobs by contract with the Mersey Railway at Birkenhead Central. On the extreme left can just be seen the Zeppelin water tank (described because of its similarity to one). This was not removed until c1969 though the depot closed in 1938. Note the top of the shear legs (far right) used for raising locos to do minor repairs. The timber buildings were hardly adequate and most of the locos stood outside at any one time. Engine No. 8 faces the camera (built by Beyer Peacock 1987-88) and No. 10, by the same builder, new in 1894, is alongside. Both were of the 0-4T type. *Photograph: J M Ryan collection.*

West Cheshire

Betley Road Station c1905 was located south of Crewe and opened on 4 July 1837 as part of the Grand Junction Railway from Birmingham to Warrington. The GJR, with the Manchester and Birmingham Railway and the London and Birmingham Railway, formed the London and North Western Railway on 16 July 1846. *Photograph: LNWR Society collection.*

The busy marshalling yards at the south end of Crewe Station have an air of silence during the coal strike of 1921. *Photograph: J M Ryan collection.*

An LNWR 4-4-0 ''Jubilee Class'' is seen here c1900 approaching Crewe from the south. On the far left can be seen the outline of the North Staffordshire Railway shed at Crewe and then the slotted post signals on the NSR line to Stoke. Further to the right are gantries controlling the entrance to Crewe station, the signals with rings referring to the slowlines. *Photograph: B S Jeuda collection.*

A view of the enlarged Crewe Station c1906 looking north, part of the ''modernisation'' of Crewe Station which started in 1896 and took ten years to complete. The modernisation took the form of avoiding goods lines to the west of the station, of extra platforms, of the burrowing of new goods lines under the mainlines to the north, and of major resignalling. *Photograph: J M Ryan collection.*

LNWR 2-4-0 ''Jumbo Class'' 652, ''Hampden'', with another locomotive of the same Class seen her at Crewe c1905. *Photograph: B S Jeuda collection.*

An LNWR 4-4-0 ''Precursor'' Class at the head of a north bound express on No. 1 platform at Crewe c1905. The three signs on the left are Refreshment Room Second Class, Refreshment Room First Class, and Dining and Tea Room. *Photograph: B S Jeuda collection.*

A view looking north from the footbridge at the north end of Crewe Station c1900 as an LNWR 2-4-0 "Jumbo" approaches Crewe Station off the Manchester line. On the left can be seen the spider bridge which carried 18 inch track of the works tramway; over this tramway spare parts and other manufactured items were brought to the station for dispatch all over the LNWR system. *Photograph: B S Jeuda collection.*

A view of Minshull Vernon Station c1920, another long closed main line station with most trains just passing through. It closed on 2 March 1942 (a rare wartime closure), a station for a small village which now, typically, is of the type fighting to keep public transport at all. The LNWR 4-4-0 heads an express towards Crewe. *Photograph: The late A G Ellis collection.*

A view of Vale Royal Arches, Northwich c1930. This was the briefly-glimpsed viaduct and vale that passengers saw as they sped south towards Crewe, on a train like this. The River Weaver (Navigation) makes a sharp bend behind the photographer and the Winsford salt mine and chemical works are soon reached. The viaduct was built by J Locke for the Grand Junction Railway and opened in 1837. *Photograph: J M Ryan collection.*

A view of Hartford Station c1905 with one of F W Webb's compound 0-8-0 goods locomotives heading south with an up goods. This station serves one of the larger villages in the district and still sees a few express trains call. On the right can be seen a covered walkway down from the main road – something that the modern day passenger has not got, plus a longer walk as well! *Photograph: B S Jeuda collection.*

A view north of Acton Bridge Station c1910. This photograph shows things prior to the up loop being built, which converted the platform for Crewe bound trains into an island one, which it remains today. The booking office sits on the bridge whence it was easy to walk down to either platform. The goods facilities were withdrawn on 4 January 1965. *Photograph: J M Ryan collection.*

Dutton Viaduct over the River Weaver. A view north of this fine structure which was part of the Grand Junction Railway main line opened to Newton Junction (now Earlestown) in 1837. It is now a listed monument but continues to carry safely West Coast Main Line traffic of a kind that its designer could never have envisaged. *Photograph: B S Jeuda collection.*

A view of the station and hotel at Preston Brook. The West Coast main line express used to thunder their way through this little station. Few trains called. The canal junction was more important. The station closed to passengers on 1 March 1948, victim of road competition, and entirely on 1 September 1958 when the goods depot closed. The hotel was presumably here because of the omnibus (coach and horses) service laid on to Runcorn in Grand Junction Railway days. *Photograph: J M Ryan collection.*

An LNWR 4-4-0 "Precursor" at the head of the mid-day mail train from Liverpool to London passing through Runcorn c1905. The section from Acton to Ditton was opened for passenger services on 1 April 1869. *Photograph: LNWR Society collection.*

A view of the Parish Church, Runcorn c1890 but of interest is the railway line which can just be seen between the Church and the River Mersey. This photograph is certainly no later than 1890 because the whole of the shoreline in this area was transformed following the construction of the Manchester Ship Canal. *Photograph: B S Jeuda collection.*

A 1905 view facing east of the Top Locks, Runcorn, on the Bridgewater Canal with Runcorn Widnes railway bridge in the background and Runcorn Station on the right. *Photograph: J M Ryan collection.*

HMS Bristol seen here c1913 watched by an interested crowd as it passes under the Runcorn-Widnes railway bridge (in the background) which was built in 1866/69 and the Widnes Transporter Bridge built between 1901 and 1905. The bridge, which cost £130,000 to build, had a span of 1,000 feet, and the four towers were 190 ft high. The car, which was suspended by cables, could carry 4 two-horse waggons and 300 passengers, and was 55 ft long. The bridge operated between 29 May 1905 and 22 July 1961. *Photograph: J M Ryan collection.*

A view of Ditton Junction, c1910 looking west towards Liverpool with the station buildings and platforms just visible in the background. The LNWR lines coming in are from the left from Crewe and Runcorn in the centre are from the Manchester and Warrington, and on the right from the Widnes Deviation Line. The postcard is interesting, because the sender writes "This is a photo of Ditton Junction, one that I took some years ago. I have marked with an X when the train left the rails and struck the buffer." *Photograph: J M Ryan collection.*

Two photographs of one of the most famous of railway accidents in the pregrouping era which took place at Ditton Junction on 17 September 1912. The entire Chester to Liverpool express train left the rails at 60 mph, and, in the ensuing damage and fires, the engineman and 13 passengers died. Seen here is the wreckage of a 2-4-0 'Jumbo' 1529, ''Cook.' The boiler which was taken back to Crewe works was the only one known to have broken its back in a derailment. *Photographs: M Ryan collection.*

The carriage works girder bridge at Crewe Works in 1882, a view looking east towards Crewe Station. The bridge line is being given its test load of six 0-6-2T locomotives. The carriage repair sheds can be seen on the righthand side beyond the bridge. *Photograph: J M Ryan collection.*

A view of the main office block of the LNWR at Crewe facing west c1904, which was built in 1876. The line in the foreground was the original Crewe to Chester Railway which was opened on 1 October 1840, and was replaced by what was known as the Deviation Line on 26 July 1868. *Photograph: B S Jeuda collection.*

LNWR "Precursor" 4-4-0 "Shooting Star" seen here coming to grief at Mill Street Bridge, Crewe, on the Chester line c1914. *Photograph: B S Jeuda collection.*

Worleston Station c1910 on the Crewe to Chester line of the LNWR. Note the ornate footbridge and the milk can whilst in the background can just be seen a crane in the goods yard, and the early LNWR signal cabin. The enamel sign on the waiting room is for Vino's Cough Cure. The station opened on 1 October 1840 (originally known as Nantwich) and closed on 1 September 1952. *Photograph: J M Ryan collection.*

Beeston Castle and Tarporley Station c1910 showing the distinct architectural features of the original promoters and builders of the Chester to Crewe Railway in 1837. The station opened on 1 October 1840 and closed on 18 April 1966. Note the cab and the water tower on the left hand side. *Photograph: J M Ryan collection.*

Postcard scenes of the stations at Chester are few and far between. Here is a comedy card which speaks for itself. *Photograph: B S Jeuda collection.*

A view of Sankey Station looking east c1910. This station was on the Skelton West Junction to Cressington Junction section of the Cheshires Lines Railway which opened for passengers on 1 August 1873. Sankey Station opened in May 1874. *Photograph: Warrington Museum & Art Gallery.*

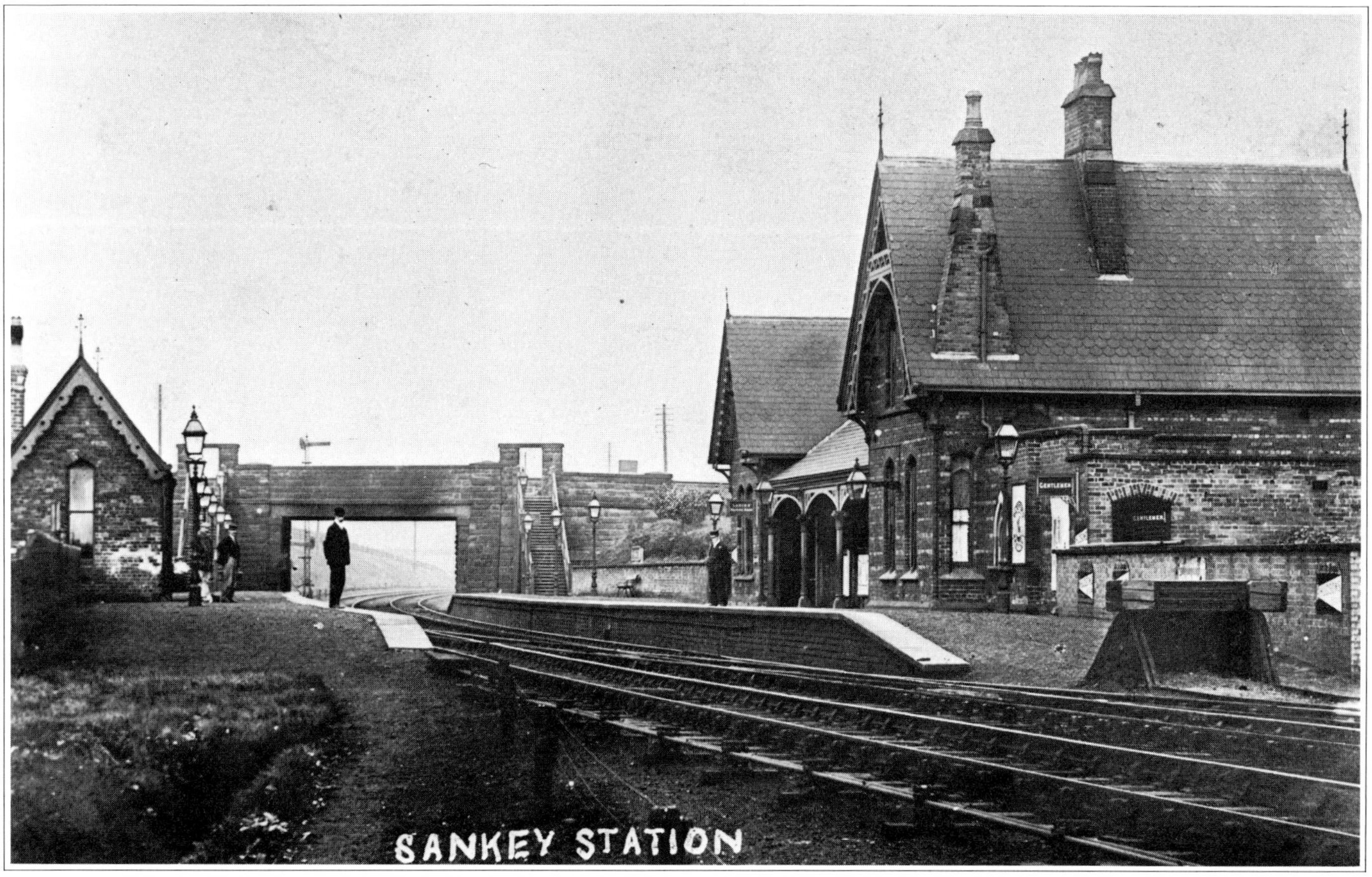

A view of the Cheshire Lines Station at Farnworth c1905 looking east towards Widnes Junction with Great Central Railway 4-2-2 Class 13 972 at the head of an express working to Liverpool. The station opened on 1 August 1873 and was renamed Widnes on May 6 1968 having been renamed Widnes (North) on 5 January 1959. *Photograph: B Hilton collection.*

Seen here at Widnes Central Station c1905 is a parade of station staff whilst a Great Central Railway 4-4-0 Class 11A 864 waits with a passenger train. The station was opened on 1 August 1879 and closed on 5 October 1964. It was located on the Great Central and Midland Joint Railway from Widnes. *Photograph: Halton Chemical Industry Museum.*

A view of Hough Green Station looking east to Manchester c1905 with a close-coupled set of Cheshire Lines stock in the foreground. Note the goods yard and loading gauge in the background. The station opened in May 1874. *Photograph: B Hilton collection.*

A view of Farnworth and Bold Station c1905 with an LNWR Coal Tank at the head of a mixed goods train. This station was on the St Helens and Runcorn Gap Railway which opened on 21 February 1833 and was absorbed by the LNWR on 29 July 1864. The station was originally named Farnworth, renamed Farnworth and Bold on 2 January 1880, and it closed on 18 June 1951. *Photograph: Halton Chemical Industry Museum.*

Norton Station and signal box c1912 viewed towards Warrington; the station closed on 1 September 1952. Only in very recent years has the area developed as part of Runcorn New Town. The signal box is a typical Birkenhead Joint example. The recently opened Runcorn East Station is close to this spot. *Photograph: J M Ryan collection*

This photograph shows Norton signal box and a musing Station Master looking at his garden. No doubt he had plenty of time in those days, the passenger train service being what it was and there were no goods facilities provided. *Photograph: J M Ryan collection.*

A view of the quayside and viaduct at Frodsham Bridge c1907. One of the highlights of a journey from Warrington to Chester is the Frodsham Viaduct which carries the line over the River Weaver (this photograph) and the Weaver Navigation. Viewed north, the mill on the right still stands today and is still served by barge traffic, which is worked from the Manchester Ship Canal. *Photograph: J M Ryan collection.*

A view of the station at Frodsham c1907. Passengers are waiting an up local towards Chester whilst two employees are more interested in the photographer! Frodsham cutting and tunnel can just be seen behind the train. Note goods facilities on both sides. The down side station building remains to this day, minus the awning. *Photograph: B S Jeuda collection.*

The underbridge at Chester Road, Frodsham, facing south c1910. The cast iron arch construction of this bridge is clearly seen as is the use of local sandstone which doubtless came from the Helsby Quarries – themselves served by a tramway at one time. *Photograph: J M Ryan collection.*

Helsby Junction viewed west c1906. The route to the east is the Chester and Warrington main line and the branch, with the LNWR train, is that from Hooton. This station has not greatly changed in 80 years – only the track, signals and trains have altered. The signal box is on the middle platform, the branch platforms being added in 1863 when the Hooton line opened.

A view of Helsby Station c1910 complementing the previous photograph, and note how the footbridge has been rebuilt – with a cover. This is surely a reflection of increasing passenger business at the station. A stopping train to Warrington and probably beyond is leaving; the train from the Hooton direction has terminated – railwaymen are standing in front of it. *Photographs: J M Ryan collection and B. S Jeuda collection.*

The track for testing Helsby Tyres. The authors had no knowledge that such an object existed until this card was found in 1982 – information is welcomed, though basically it is reasonably clear what happened. The vehicle would appear to be electrically powered by means of the cable supply. *Photograph: J M Ryan collection.*

A view of Ince and Elton Station c1905 towards Helsby, another station with the Birkenhead Joint Railway architectural "house style". Then very much in the country, industry has spread south east and now surrounds this station. The "express" would appear to be a goods and the locomotive one of the famed "Dean Goods" engines. The signals are LNWR standard Crewe types. On this line, the two joint owning railways each left their mark in a distinctive way. GWR engines were still running on the Wirral till the late 1950's. *Photograph: M Day collection.*

A view of Mickle Trafford Station c1910. This station, opened on 18 December 1850 and closed on 2 April 1951, is now impossible to trace. Mickle Trafford was then very small and the very recent expansion of population came far too late to save the station. A staff of three would be considered exhorbitant today at such a place – even including the signal man. *Photograph: E Talbot collection.*

The LNWR line from Warrington to Widnes is seen here c1906 running close to the Sankey Canal at Penketh. Note, on the left of the picture, the LNWR slotted post signal. *Photograph: J M Ryan collection.*

A view of the LNWR station, Fiddlers Ferry and Penketh, c1904. This station was on the section which opened from Garston to Warrington on 1 May 1854. The station closed on 2 January 1950. *Photograph: J M Ryan collection.*

Cuddington Station looking east towards Northwich c1905. The station opened on 1 September 1869 and the section from Cuddington Junction to Winsford and Over (including the branch to Winsford Salt Works) opened on 1 June 1870. *Photograph: B S Jeuda collection.*

A military detachment at Cuddington during the First World War. Note the station nameboard, which indicates the need to change for Whitegate and Winsford, and the cast-iron toilet in the background. *Photograph: Heyday Publishing Company.*

A view of Whitegate Station looking east towards Winsford and Over c1910. Note the different patterns of flowers in the station gardens. The station opened for passengers on 1 July 1870, closed for passengers on 1 January 1931 and for goods on 4 November 1963. *Photograph: J Chesworth collection.*

The line from Cuddington Junction to Winsford and Over and from Falk's Junction to Winsford Salt Works was opened on 1 June 1870 and closed on 1 June 1958. Winsford was a major salt producing area, and the volume of salt traffic passing over the Cuddington branch was substantial. *Photograph: B S Jeuda collection.*

Winsford and Over was the terminus of the branch from Cuddington. Seen here c1900 is a Sacré designed Class 12A 2-4-0 built by the Manchester, Sheffield and Lincolnshire Railway in 1885. The station opened for passenger traffic on 1 July 1870 and closed on 1 January 1931. *Photograph: Winsford Historical Society.*

A fine parade of station staff c1905 outside a freshly painted Delamere signal box. On the right can be seen signals to a standard Cheshire Lines design. Note the size of the spectacle on the home signal. *Photograph: B S Jeuda collection.*

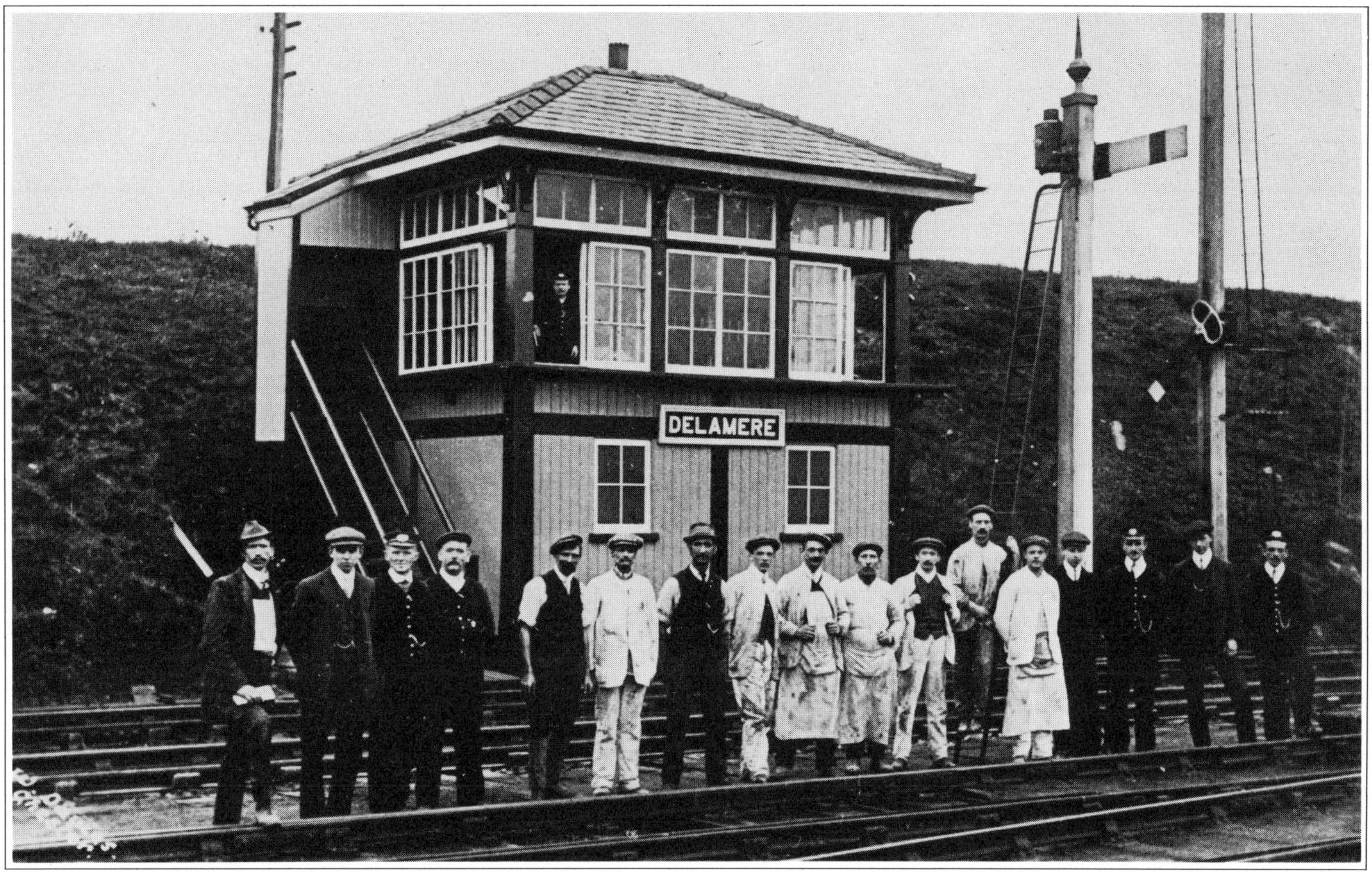

Delamere Station looking east to Manchester c1905. The station staff can be seen on the right while, on the left, the look out man is holding his flags. *Photograph: J M Ryan collection.*

The rear of a goods train coming off the Helsby branch and passing through Mouldsworth c1905. Midland Railway and Great Western Railway wagons can be clearly seen. Note the stone waiting room. *Photograph: J M Ryan collection.*

A view of the exterior of Mouldsworth Station c1905. Note two tall home signals on the far left of the picture. The home signal on the left is for the line to Chester Northgate opened as the Chester and West Cheshire Junction Railway which was absorbed by the Cheshire Lines on 10 August 1866 prior to the opening of the line. The home signal of the right is for the line to Helsby Junction which opened on 22 June 1870 as part of West Cheshire Railway's line from Helsby and Alvanley to Northwich, which Railway formed part of the Cheshire Lines and opened on 5 July 1865. *Photograph: B S Jeuda collection.*

A view looking towards Chester of Mickle Trafford Station in 1911 with an excursion for New Brighton about to depart. The station opened for passengers in December 1889 and closed for passengers on 12 February 1951. *Photograph: A Willis collection.*

The familiar scene of members of a permanent way gang cleaning the points under snowy conditions. This picture was taken on the Cheshire lines at Chester in 1921, with the spire of the Cathedral prominent in the background. *Photograph: B S Jeuda collection.*

A well-known LNWR official postcard showing an LNWR 2-4-0 ''Jumbo'' c1900 crossing the Shropshire Union Canal at Chester. *Photograph: B S Jeuda collection.*

A view of the bridge at Saltney Station in 1904 with a local tram in the foreground. Saltney Station was on the Shrewsbury, Oswestry and Chester Junction Railway which in turn was amalgamated with the Great Western Railway on 1 September 1854. The station opened on 4 November 1846 and closed on 12 September 1960. *Photograph: B S Jeuda collection.*

The Eaton Hall railway of the Duke of Westminster was constructed between 1884 and 1886 to connect Eaton Hall, at Eccleston near Chester, to the Great Western Railway at Balderton, a distance of three miles. The prime function of the line was the conveyance of estate produce to the GWR, and the carriage of coal on the return journey, but a certain amount of pleasure operation took place. Seen here c1910 is the 0-4-0T ''Katie'' operating on the 1 foot 3 inch gauge. *Photograph: J M Ryan collection.*

A Great Western Railway bus seen here c1905 at Farndon. The GWR ran a bus service between Wrexham and neighbouring villages. *Photograph: B S Jeuda collection.*

A view of Malpas Station c1905 which was situated on the LNWR branch line from Tattenhall Junction to Whitchurch and which opened on 1 October 1872. It was one of Cheshire's least known and least used lines but this station survived until 16 September 1957. *Photograph: J M Ryan collection.*

The Nantwich and Market Drayton Railway was incorporated in 1861 and opened on 20 October 1863. The Railway was amalgamated with the Great Western Railway on 1 July 1897. Seen here c1905 is the station staff on parade at Audlem. The station closed on 9 September 1963. *Photograph: B S Jeuda collection.*

Mr Edmund Driver organised a series of cheese trains between Cheshire and Bradford, and between July 1907 and December 1908, 6 special chartered trains, carrying 7,804 cheeses which weighed 18 tons, were run by Mr Driver. This is a photo of the Christmas cheese train of 1907 which carried 1,257 cheeses, weighing 18 tons, and valued at £1,900. This special train also carried practically all the first prize and gold medal winners at nearly all the great Cheshire Christmas cheese shows, but also carried valuable trophies in the shape of silver challenge cups and gold and silver medals – indeed this was the first time the trophies had been allowed out of Cheshire. *Photograph: B S Jeuda collection.*

Above is seen one of the numerous Special Trains about to leave the heart of the Cheshire Cheese Industry with Cheese solely for Driver's Depots.

Wrenbury Station c1905 was located on the Crewe to Shrewsbury line of the LNWR. The station opened on 2 September 1858 and closed for passenger services on 19 September 1966. *Photograph: LNWR Society collection.*

OFFICIAL

RAILWAY MAP OF THE

LANCASHIRE & CHESHIRE DISTRICTS

PREPARED AND PUBLISHE[D]

RAILWAY CLEARING H[OUSE]

LONDON

1913

STATUTE MILES.

The distances in[dic]ated on this Map are approximate: their

Drawn and engraved by J. & W. Emslie

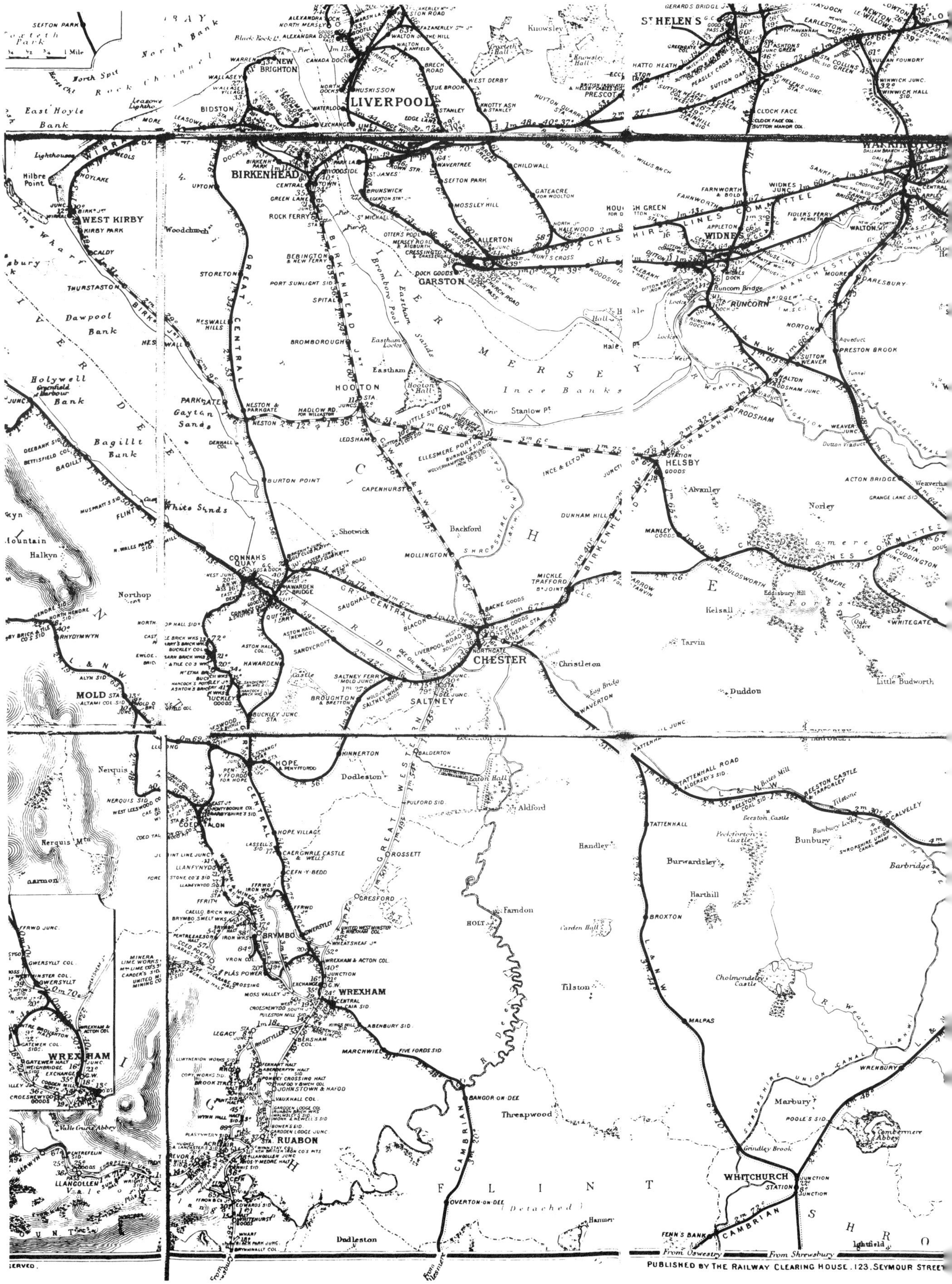

PUBLISHED BY THE RAILWAY CLEARING HOUSE, 123, SEYMOUR STREET

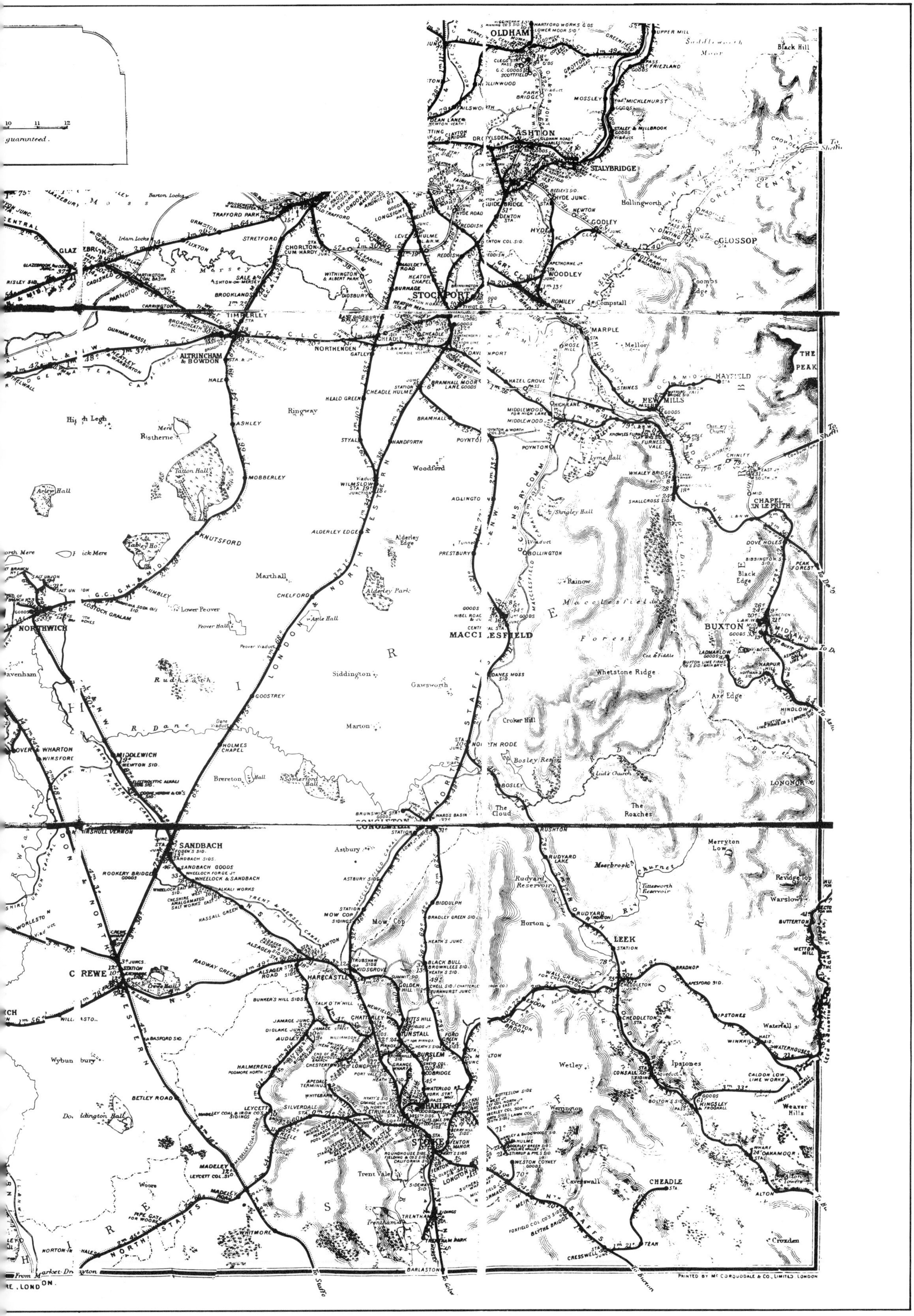

OLDHAM
ASHTON
STALYBRIDGE
GLOSSOP
Black Hill
Hollingworth
MOSSLEY
GODLEY
HYDE
WOODLEY
ROMILEY
STOCKPORT
CHEADLE
TIMPERLEY
ALTRINCHAM & BOWDON
NORTHENDEN
MARPLE
Mellor
NEW MILLS
HAYFIELD
THE PEAK
CHAPEL EN LE FRITH
WHALEY BRIDGE
BUXTON
Lyme Hall
POYNTON
BRAMHALL
HANDFORTH
WILMSLOW
ALDERLEY EDGE
Woodford
PRESTBURY
BOLLINGTON
MACCLESFIELD
Rainow
Macclesfield Forest
Whetstone Ridge
Axe Edge
CHELFORD
KNUTSFORD
MOBBERLEY
ASHLEY
Ringway
Tatton Hall
Arley Hall
Tabley Ho
Marthall
Lower Peover
NORTHWICH
LOSTOCK GRALAM
PLUMBLEY
Siddington
Gawsworth
Marton
GOOSTREY
HOLMES CHAPEL
Brereton
MIDDLEWICH
WINSFORD
Croker Hill
Bosley Res
BOSLEY
The Cloud
The Roaches
LONGNOR
CONGLETON
SANDBACH
Astbury
Mow Cop
BIDDULPH
RUDYARD LAKE
Rudyard Reservoir
Horton
LEEK
CHEDDLETON
Ipstones
CREWE
Crewe Hall
ALSAGER ROAD
HARECASTLE
KIDSGROVE
TUNSTALL
BURSLEM
HANLEY
STOKE
NEWCASTLE
SILVERDALE
AUDLEY
Wybunbury
BETLEY ROAD
Doddington Hall
MADELEY
WHITMORE
Trent Vale
Trentham
BARLASTON
Wetley
Caverswall
CHEADLE
ALTON
Croxden
OAKAMOOR
Weaver Hills
Waterfall
BLYTHE BRIDGE
CRESSWELL
NORTH STAFFS
LONDON & NORTH WESTERN
Warslow
Revidge Top
Merryton Low
Tittesworth Reservoir
Meerbrook
R. Mersey
R. Dane
PRINTED BY McCORQUODALE & CO. LIMITED LONDON

A view of Nantwich Station in 1912, with Mr Ratcliffe in the centre of the group.
Photograph: Mr F L Ratcliffe collection.

A view of Saughall Station c1905. This station was on a section of the Great Central Railway from Chester to Hawarden Bridge which opened on 31 March 1890 and which connected with the Hawarden Bridge to Bidston line. The station which opened on 16 March 1896 and closed on 1 February 1954. *Photograph: B S Jeuda collection.*

The Manchester, South Junction and Altrincham Railway was authorised in 1845 to link Manchester with Altrincham, and arising out of various mergers in 1846 involving the London and North Western Railway and the Manchester, Sheffield and Lincolnshire Railway, the MSJAR became jointly owned by these two companies. An exterior view of Sale Station c1904 with a horse cab just visible on the right hand side. The station opened on 20 July 1849. *Photograph: J M Ryan collection.*

Sale Station c1904 looking west to Manchester. *Photograph: B S Jeuda collection.*

Two contrasting photographs taken from the footbridge at Timperley Station and looking towards Sale and with the Bridgewater Canal on the left. In the top photograph, c1910, can be seen a Manchester to Chester express, whilst the bottom photograph, c1935, shows a Manchester to Altrincham passenger train passing under the gantries of the 1500 volt DC overhead system which was introduced on 11 May 1931. The signals in both photographs are different and note the new housing on the right hand side of the lower photograph. The station opened on 20 July 1849. *Photographs: B S Jeuda collection. J M Ryan collection.*

The line from Stockport Portwood to Northenden and beyond was opened on 1 December 1865 as part of the Stockport, Timperley and Altrincham Junction Railway. Northenden Station was opened on 1 February 1866 and closed for passengers on 30 November 1964. Note the advertisement on the left hand side of the ''New'' Midland Hotel, Manchester, described as ''one of the finest hotels in Europe''. *Photograph: B S Jeuda collection.*

Baguley Station c1905 looking east towards Stockport with the signal man posing outside his box. Note the ornate barge boards and the well kept garden. The station opened on 1 February 1866 and closed for passengers on 30 November 1964. *Photograph: J M Ryan collection.*

A view of Skelton Junction c1905 looking west towards Liverpool. From left to right are, firstly the LNWR line to Warrington (the former Warrington and Stockport Railway), secondly the CLR to Glazebrook and Warrington, thirdly sidings, and fourthly the CLR connection with the Manchester South Junction and Altrincham Railway at Deansgate Junction which passed under the other first two railway lines. Just to the right of the footbridge, the lighter coloured fencing shows where went the Great Central Railway's spur from Skelton North Junction to Timperley Junction (opened in 1879 and closed in 1903). *Photograph: J M Ryan collection.*

A view of Altrincham and Bowdon Station c1905. When the MSJAR opened in July 1849 there were separate stations at Altrincham and at Bowdon. A new station was built later, and it opened on 2 April 1881. *Photograph: B S Jeuda collection.*

A view of Hale Station taken c1912. This station was opened on 12 May 1862 and was originally called Bowdon Peel Causeway. It was renamed Peel Causeway on 1 January 1899 and again renamed as Hale on 1 May 1902. *Photograph: B S Jeuda collection.*

Hale Station c1910 as a Chester to Manchester passenger train pulls in, drawn by a Great Central 4-4-2T 357. Note the large number of businessmen waiting whilst on the right can be seen the officers of R Edgell & Co, Coal and Coke Merchants. *Photograph: Hale Civic Society.*

Mobberley Station c1910 with the Station Master's house in the background. The station opened on 12 May 1862. *Photograph: B S Jeuda collection.*

Knutsford Station looking west c1905 with typical Cheshire Lines Platform awnings of dark and light brown. The station opened on 12 May 1862. Note the water tower on the right hand side. *Photograph: B S Jeuda collection.*

A view c1902 thought to be of the chemical works of Davis' Chlorine Processes Ltd. just to the west of Lostock Gralam Station. Just to the right of the chimney can be seen a Cheshire Lines signal box. *Photograph: B S Jeuda collection.*

Northwich Station c1905 looking towards Chester. The original station was opened on 1 January 1863 as part of the Cheshire Midland Railways, but was closed in May 1868 to make way for a second Northwich Station, on the West Cheshire Railway from Northwich to Helsby and Alvanley. The new station opened for goods, on 1 September 1869, and for passengers on 22 June 1870. *Photograph: B S Jeuda collection.*

A front view of Northwich Station c1910, showing, on the left, the entrance to the goods yard and, on the right, Reece Brooks, photographers, "electric studio". *Photograph: B S Jeuda collection.*

One of the most important engineering works on the Cheshire Lines Railway is the viaduct between Hartford and Northwich which carries the railway over the rivers Dane and Weaver, and over the Weaver Canal. It consists of 48 stone arches and two wrought iron girder bridges, giving a total length of around 725 yards. The viaduct provides the backdrop for two Salt Union barges, "Two Sisters" and "National," and the Steamboat "Pacific". *Photograph: B S Jeuda collection.*

The line from Northwich Junction to the Brunner Mond's works at Winnington was opened on 1 June 1870, and carried substantial traffic, to the works, of limestone from the Peak District, and of coal from North Staffordshire and elsewhere. The lines snakes through Northwich and is seen here c1905 passing over Chester Road. *Photograph: B S Jeuda collection*.

A view of Hartford and Greenbank Station c1906 looking east towards Northwich. In the background can just be seen the construction activity for the spur line from the East to the North junctions (and thence to the Winnington branch) which opened in 1907. *Photograph: B S Jeuda collection*.

The Partington Coaling Basin on the canal was linked into the railway system with coal tips in use on both sides of the Canal; by 1920 there were 24 miles of track. This view c1920 looking east to Manchester, with the Irlam Viaduct in the background, shows the rail sidings leading to the coal tips on the south side of the Canal. *Photograph: B S Jeuda collection.*

A view of Padgate Station looking east to Manchester. The station was opened on 1 September 1873 and the design of its station buildings is standard Cheshire Lines architecture. Note the new cattle dock on the right hand side. *Photograph: Warrington Museum and Art Gallery.*

A view of Warrington Central Station looking west c1915. This station was opened on 1 August 1873, initially on a loopline, as part of the line from Skelton Junction to Cressington (near Garston). *Photograph: B S Jeuda collection.*

A view of the coal yard c1908 at the LNWR Station of Broadheath near Altrincham. In the background can be seen the station platform, and beyond that Richards and Company's Atlantic Works. Broadheath was on the Warrington and Stockport Railway (absorbed into the LNWR in August 1859) and the station opened on 1 November 1853. The station closed on 10 September 1962. *Photograph: J M Ryan collection.*

Salt was discovered in Lymm around 1901 and Heatley Salt Works, seen here on 22 April 1914, was the first of three works to be built in the area. It was located to the west of Heatley and Warburton Station and had a connection to the line. Around the time of the First World War, there was a plan to load ships and salt on the Manchester Ship Canal; land for a railway was bought and a bridge was built over the River Bollin but the project came to nought. *Photograph: J M Ryan collection.*

Heatley and Warburton Station c1905. When the line opened on 1 November 1853, there were separate stations at Heatley and at Warburton, but in November 1856, Warburton was renamed Dunham (later Dunham Massey) and Heatley was renamed Heatley and Warburton. The station closed on 10 September 1962. *Photograph: J M Ryan collection.*

A view of Lymm Station looking towards Altrincham c1905 with the level crossing in the background. The station opened on 1 November 1853 and closed on 10 September 1962. *Photograph: Warrington Museum and Art Gallery.*

An aerial view, probably taken in the 1930's, of Lymm Station and of the surrounding buildings. Note the footbridge which is not present in the earlier photograph. *Photograph: J M Ryan collection.*

The building of the Manchester Ship Canal necessitated the deviation of the original line from Broadheath to Warrington near Latchford. This view c1905 shows the footbridge over the new line at Wash Lane, Latchford, whilst in the background can just be seen an industrial locomotive on duty on the Manchester Ship Canal Railway. *Photograph: B S Jeuda collection.*

The Manchester Ship Canal runs for 35½ miles from Eastham, where it leaves the River Mersey, almost to the centre of Manchester. The construction took place between 1887 and 1894 and was beset by financial problems and by the vagaries of the weather. The Canal was opened on 21 May 1894. This view c1910 from the Cheshire banks, with the River Mersey coming in from the right, shows a Great Central Railway 4-4-0 working a Manchester to Liverpool passenger train across the Irlam Viaduct over the Canal. The original line was opened on 2 September 1873, but the construction of the Canal required a new and higher route; this was known as the Irlam deviation and opened for passenger traffic on 26 March 1893. *Photograph: J M Ryan collection.*

A view of Cadishead Viaduct c1910 looking towards Partington, which carried the Cheshire Lines branch from Skelton Junction to Glazebrook Junction. This section was opened on 1 August 1873, but the construction of the Canal required a 2½ mile deviation line to be built to get the necessary height over it. The deviation was opened completely for passenger and goods traffic on 29 May 1893. *Photograph: J M Ryan collection.*

A view c1910 of the toll bridge at Warburton over the Canal. The railway line on the left belongs to the Manchester Ship Canal Company Railway; this Railway was the largest privately owned railway in Britain, with 75 locomotives, almost 2,700 wagons, and 231 miles of track. The railway was split into several isolated sections, the line at Warburton being part of the section that went from the docks at Salford to Latchford (Warrington). *Photograph: B S Jeuda collection.*

A convoy of tugs and boats at the Latchford bridge which carried the LNWR line from Manchester (via Sale) and from Stockport (via Skelton) to Warrington. The line on the left belongs to the Canal Railway. *Photograph: J M Ryan collection.*

This postcard, an 1891 view, shows in impressive detail the actual construction of the Canal at Latchford. The steam excavator on the bottom left is clearly visible, whilst in the centre can be seen the contractors' railway partly under water, and numerous loaded trucks can be seen. In the background can be seen the newly built LNWR deviation line, No. 3, which replaced the existing line. *Photograph: Warrington Museum and Art Gallery.*

A view of the original Latchford Station to the left of the Canal cutting looking east to Manchester, c1891. Beyond the trestle bridge in the foreground can be seen part of what was to become the Knutsford Road swing road bridge over the Canal. The new LNWR line from Manchester, and from Stockport, to Warrington is in the background. *Photograph: Warrington Museum and Art Gallery.*

A photograph of the original Latchford Station c1889 looking east towards Stockport. The nearest level crossing was at Grappenhall Road, whilst the distant crossing was at Knutsford Road. The station was closed on 8 July 1893 on the opening of the deviation line over the canal and a new Latchford Station built; that station in turn closed on 10 September 1962. *Photograph: Warrington Museum and Art Gallery.*

East Cheshire

The first section of the Manchester and Birmingham Railway opened from Manchester (Travis Street) to Stockport on 4 June 1840. Heaton Chapel was the first station in Cheshire on that section. *Photograph: B S Jeuda collection.*

An interesting card to commemorate the piano playing feat, in Stockport in October 1906, of M L Napolean Bird for the benefit of the LNWR Employees Brass Band. *Photograph: B S Jeuda collection.*

A view of Stockport viaduct just north of Stockport Edgeley Station looking towards Manchester. The viaduct was 600 yards long and carried the rails at a height of 111 feet above the bed of the River Mersey. There were 22 arches, each of 63 foot span, and 4 smaller arches in the abutments. Work commenced on 10 March 1839 and was completed on 21 December 1840, with the first train passing over on 30 July 1841. The viaduct was subsequently widened in 1889 to carry four tracks. *Photograph: Stockport Borough Libraries.*

A delightful picture of an LNWR horse and cab outside Stockport Edgeley Station c1905. *Photograph: J M Ryan collection.*

LNWR 2-2-2 ''Problem'' Class locomotive 1429, ''Alfred Paget,'' seen here at Stockport Station, c1900. This locomotive was one of sixty of this class built at Crewe between 1859 and 1865. *Photograph: B S Jeuda collection.*

C Class 2-4-0 North Staffordshire Railway locomotive, ''Colin Minton Campbell'', at the head of a local passenger train at Stockport working the service between Manchester (London Road) and Macclesfield c1900. *Photograph: B S Jeuda Collection.*

A delightful picture at Cheadle Hulme Station of Edwardian gentlemen and ladies, in all their finery, leaving the platform on the Stockport to Wilmslow line c1908. Note the various station signs, bench and gas lamps. Advertising signs can be seen for Pears soap, Sages shopfittings, Mazawattee tea, and Arighi Bianchi (house furnishers of Macclesfield). *Photograph: B S Jeuda collection.*

Poynton Coal Junction signal box in the foreground and Poynton Station in the background c1900. The line to the left of the signal box ran to the Poynton Colliery railway network, and was opened to coal traffic on 9 June 1845 as the first part of the Manchester and Birmingham Railway line to Macclesfield – from Cheadle Hulme to Prince Pit. This station was the second station to be built in Poynton and was opened on 1 August 1887; the original station at Midway, half a mile further south, was opened on 24 November 1845 and lasted until the later station opened. *Photograph: J M Ryan collection.*

Poynton Station looking north to Stockport c1905. Note the tall chimney of the Brick Works in the background, whilst to the right of the signal box can be seen the complex of buildings which formed the Gas Works built in 1845; both Works were owned by Poynton and Worth Collieries. *Photograph: J M Ryan collection.*

The first records to show coal mining in Poynton date back to 1589. The operation of the Poynton Collieries by Lord Vernon from 1832 saw rapid expansion of production which in 1831 with peak output being reached of 243,673 tons in 1859 amounted to 86,514 tons. This was assisted initially by the Macclesfield Canal, opened on 18 November 1831, and later by the Manchester and Birmingham Railway in 1845, and the Macclesfield, Bollington and Marple Railway in 1869. The collieries closed on 30 August 1935, with 250 men being made redundant. A view of Park Pits, 1930. Note the tall engine house, Oval Pit and lower engine house, and Lawrance pit. *Photograph: J M Ryan collection.*

Anson Road level crossing, a view towards Anson Pit c1905. *Photograph: J M Ryan collection.*

A turn of the century view of Adlington Station facing south. The station design is similar to the later Poynton Station, but different to the Manchester and Birmingham Railway stations which also opened on 24 November 1845. *Photograph: J M Ryan collection.*

All the power and romance of travel by rail can be seen as a double-headed Manchester to London express powers through Prestbury c1914. The station building on the left was built by the Manchester and Birmingham Railway and is the only MBR building to survive as a working station. The station was opened on 24 November 1845. An LNWR 5 foot 6 inch tank is seen here piloting a 4-4-0 'Benbow' class compound. *Photograph: J M Ryan collection.*

The London and North Western Railway Parcels Receiving Office at Park Green, Macclesfield, c1905, can be seen to the right of the picture. *Photograph: B S Jeuda collection.*

Cheadle Hulme was an important junction with the Manchester and Birmingham Railway, later the LNWR line to Macclesfield, on the left and the MBR line to Wilmslow and Crewe in the foreground. The original Cheadle (Cheadle Hulme) station which was a quarter of a mile to the south of the present station was opened on 10 May 1842 and closed on 24 November 1845. This station was renamed Cheadle Hulme on 1 March 1866 to avoid confusion with the newly opened LNWR station on the Stockport to Northenden line. *Photograph: J M Ryan collection.*

Railway station staff have traditionally taken great pride in station gardens. This photograph of Handforth Station shows the imaginative and delightful combination of bushes, plants and ballast to make a delightful scene. This station, which had staggered platforms, was originally built by the Manchester and Birmingham Railway to link Manchester with Crewe, and was opened on 10 May 1842. Note the ornate footbridge in the background. *Photograph: B S Jeuda collection.*

Wilmslow Station, which opened on 10 May 1842, c1905 showing also the coal depot of the Poynton and Worth Collieries; the private owner wagons are all lettered, "Poynton Collieries, Lord Vernon." At the entrance to the coal depot can be seen the coal office and the bed-plate of the weighing machine, and, on the far left, the entrance to the LNWR goods yard. *Photograph: J M Ryan collection.*

Wilmslow Station c1910 was rebuilt and enlarged in 1909 for the opening of the Wilmslow to Levenshulme Railway ("the Styal line"). This photograph should be compared with the previous one, and the most obvious change being the removal of Lord Vernon's coal yard. Note the water column in the background. *Photograph: Cheshire Libraries and Museums Department.*

The Royal Train passing through Wilmslow on 14 July 1913 taking King George V and Queen Mary back to London after a visit to Lancashire. At the head of the train are two 4-4-0 "George V" Class locomotives, "Loyalty" and "St George, both of which were built three months earlier in April 1913. Note the elegance of the royal saloons, behind which can just be seen the elevated signal box and a partial outline of the goods shed. *Photograph: B S Jeuda collection.*

Alderley Edge Station c1905, looking towards Wilmslow, was opened on 10 May 1842 (Edge added January 1876). Alderley Edge was an important commuter station from the time it was opened and the coming of the railway encouraged many textile magnates to leave Manchester for the delights of the Cheshire plains. Many elegant homes were built from the mid 1840's and the LNWR initially offered free season tickets to encourage people to move out from Manchester. Note the ornate passenger footbridge, the Queen's Hotel in the background, and the carriage loading dock on the right hand side. *Photograph: J M Ryan collection.*

The copper mines at Alderley Edge showing the narrow gauge tramway. Copper had been mined at Alderley intermittently from 1693 to 1919, with the principal period of operations between 1857 and 1877. In 1912 the mines reopened and activity on a small scale continued until 1919. During this period, the haulage incline at West Mine was constructed, and this photograph shows the incline and West Mine entrance. *Photograph: B S Jeuda collection.*

Chelford Station looking north c1905. Note the milk loading dock on the left hand side whilst a windmill can just be seen to the left of the leaning telegraph pole. Beyond the station staff can just be seen the water tower. Chelford, although a village of a few hundred people, was strategically located roughly half way between Macclesfield and Knutsford. The station was a centre for agriculture and coal traffic for neighbouring villages, and was for many years the collection and distribution point for the Royal Mail. *Photograph: J M Ryan collection.*

The famous Chelford railway accident on 22 December 1894 when 13 people were killed and a further 48 injured. The train was the 4.15pm Manchester (London Road) to Euston express which collided with wagons that were being shunted in the goods yard. Behind the wrecked carriages can be seen the wooden goods shed and the water tower, and, behind the water tower, the Chelford engine shed. *Photograph: B S Jeuda collection.*

The LNWR viaduct over the River Dane, just north of Holmes Chapel, was one of the most impressive features of railway engineering and architecture in Cheshire. It was 1,794 feet in length, with 23 arches each of 63 feet span. *Photograph: B S Jeuda collection.*

A view of Sandbach Station looking south, c1905, with the tall LNWR signal box in the background. This station opened on 10 May 1842 and was an important junction with the LNWR line from Northwich and Middlewich which opened in November 1867, and with the NSR line to Harecastle which was finally completed in December 1866. *Photograph: V R Anderson collection.*

An aerial view taken in the late 1920's of the Palmer, Mann Works of Sifta Salt, located at Rookery Bridge approximately one mile south of Sandbach station. The works were served by sidings off the main line. Note the mounds of salt all round the works. *Photograph: J M Ryan collection.*

Davenport Station c1905 looking towards Stockport with an approaching Buxton passenger train. The advertising notices on the left hand side are for K Boots and Shoes, Workmen's tickets, the Manchester Evening Chronicle, Norway Fjords, the Daily Dispatch, Hudson's Soap and excursions to Belle Vue and to Blackpool, North Wales and the Isle of Man. *Photograph: B S Jeuda collection.*

Hazel Grove Station looking north towards Stockport c1905. *Photograph: B S Jeuda collection.*

Norbury Crossing, Middlewood c1905 looking towards Stockport. An LNWR "Precursor" 4-4-2T heads a six-carriage Manchester to Buxton passenger train. This road and foot crossing, between Higher Poynton and the A6 road at High Lane, still exists. *Photograph: B S Jeuda collection.*

A view of Middlewood Station c1910 looking towards Hazel Grove. The bridge in the centre of the view carried the Macclesfield Bollington and Marple Railway from Macclesfield Central to Marple Rose Hill, and to Manchester, over the LNWR line from Manchester to Buxton. A "Precursor" Tank enters the station as a painter goes about his business. To the left of the bridge was Middlewood Station on the MB&MR (which was an exchange station with the LNWR station, both of which were opened on 1 April 1879). *Photograph: : B S Jeuda collection.*

A view of Disley Station looking towards New Mills c1905, showing the original station buildings. The bridge in the background carries the main A6 road between Stockport and Buxton over the railway line. Disley had a separate LNWR goods station about ¾ mile to the south. *Photograph: J M Ryan collection.*

A later view of Disley Station c1930 looking towards New Mills. Note the difference in architecture compared with the previous photograph. The original Disley station was burnt down c1912. *Photograph: B S Jeuda collection.*

New Mills Station c1905 looking towards Whaley Bridge. In the background can just be seen the large goods warehouse. The station was opened on 9 June 1857, and was renamed New Mills (Newtown) on 2 June 1924. *Photograph: V R Anderson collection.*

Furness Vale Station looking north c1905. Note the latticed footbridge in the background. *Photograph: J M Ryan collection.*

A view of Whaley Bridge Station looking north c1905. Whaley Bridge was the terminus of the Stockport, Disley and Whaley Bridge Railway which, though nominally independent, was almost entirely financed by the LNWR. The line was opened officially on 28 May 1857 and passenger services commenced a few days later on 9 June. Whaley Bridge had its own locomotive shed. *Photograph: B S Jeuda collection.*

A view of Whaley Bridge c1905 looking west towards Macclesfield. The railway line in the foreground is the former Cromford and High Peak Railway which linked Cromford in Derbyshire with the Peak Forest Canal at Whaley Bridge; the CHPR warehouse can just be seen on the right hand side. This railway was opened in its full length on 6 July 1831, and the last section finally closed on 2 October 1967. Shallcross yard at Whaley Bridge closed on 30 January 1965. In the centre of the picture can be seen the LNWR line and Whaley Bridge Station, including water tower, goods shed, station buildings and signal box. *Photograph: J M Ryan collection.*

The Wilmslow to Levenshulme Railway (the Styal line) was constructed by the LNWR to relieve train congestion at Stockport. The line was 9 miles 36 chains long, and produced a saving in distance between Manchester and Wilmslow of a mere quarter mile. This view shows the approach of the first passenger train into Gatley Station on opening day, 1 May 1909. *Photograph: J M Ryan collection.*

This photograph of Heald Green Station looking north to Manchester was taken very shortly after the Styal line was opened. Note the newness of the various station buildings and signs. *Photograph: Stockport Borough Libraries.*

Two photographs of Styal Station looking north to Manchester. This one shows the approach of the first train which was worked by double-headed LNWR 2-4-2T locomotives; note the freshly ballasted track.

Staff at the newly built station passing the time of day. The poster advertises the Manchester and Wilmslow New Line. *Photograph: J M Ryan collection and B Hilton collection.*

The front of Cheadle LNWR Station c1910 with a horse drawn bus from Cheadle to Palatine Road (south Manchester). Cheadle was located on a section from Stockport to Northdenden which was opened on 1 August 1866, and provided the LNWR with a route, running over a short section of Cheshire Lines, from Stockport to Warrington and Liverpool. Cheadle station had a relatively short life closing on 1 January 1917, though the line is still open for mineral traffic. *Photograph: J M Ryan collection.*

A view of Cheadle Station c1905 looking towards Stockport with an LNWR 0-6-2T at the head of a 7-coach set. *Photograph: B S Jeuda collection.*

An aerial view of Macclesfield c1922; in the centre of the picture can be seen the coal yard of the North Staffordshire Railway, the recently constructed cattle pens, and the extension of the up platform at Macclesfield Hibel Road Station. The railway line to the left goes from Macclesfield Central Station (at the top of the picture) to Bollington, whilst at the bottom of the picture can be seen the joint LNWR/NSR goods yard and shed. *Photograph: B S Jeuda collection.*

A photograph showing the departure of the 7th Cheshire Territorials from Macclesfield Hibel Road Station during the First World War. *Photograph: B S Jeuda collection.*

Two photographs taken of Buxton Road, Macclesfield, the top taken in 1905 and the bottom in 1935, provide the opportunity to compare changes in buildings and landscape over a 30 year period. The NSR signal gantry shows no change although the 1935 photograph shows the newly constructed London Midland and Scottish Railway Macclesfield Central signal box, opened in 1934. Note the Hovis publicity works on the right hand side which dominates the skyline. *Photographs: B S Jeuda collection.*

Macclesfield Central Station c1905 looking towards Congleton. Behind the station can just be seen the Mortar Mill signal box and water tower. This station was opened on 1 July 1873 and was owned by the Macclesfield Bollington and Marple Railway. *Photograph: J M Ryan collection.*

A view of railway activity in Macclesfield c1905. In the foreground on the right can be seen firstly the roof of Hibel Road Station, jointly owned by the LNWR and NSR) and secondly the roof of the NSR engine shed; the station and shed were opened in 1849. In the foreground left can be seen the original MB&MR station, opened in 1869 and closed in 1873, and behind it the extensive MB&MR coal yard. *Photograph: G K Fox collection.*

A view of Bollington Station c1905 looking towards Macclesfield. The station buildings were built to a standard North Staffordshire Railway design, and the plans used to construct Bollington Station were those which had been used for building Silverdale Station on the Stoke to Market Drayton line. Behind the signal can just be seen the goods shed and goods yard. The station opened on 2 August 1869 and closed on 5 January 1970. *Photograph: J M Ryan collection.*

One of the many comedy cards published at the turn of the century. *Photograph: B S Jeuda collection.*

Station staff at Middlewood c1919. Behind can be seen two poster boards headed up with the initials GC&NSRC – the Great Central and North Staffordshire Railway Companies. The poster on the left advertised Great Central excursions to Southport, Liverpool and Chester while the one on the right advertises excursions to Rudyard Lake, the Anglers paradise. This station was opened on 1 April 1879, together with the nearby Middlewood Station on the LNWR line from Stockport to Buxton, to provide passenger interchange facilities between both lines. This station was renamed Middlewood Higher on 25 July 1951 and closed on 7 November 1960. *Photograph: J M Ryan collection.*

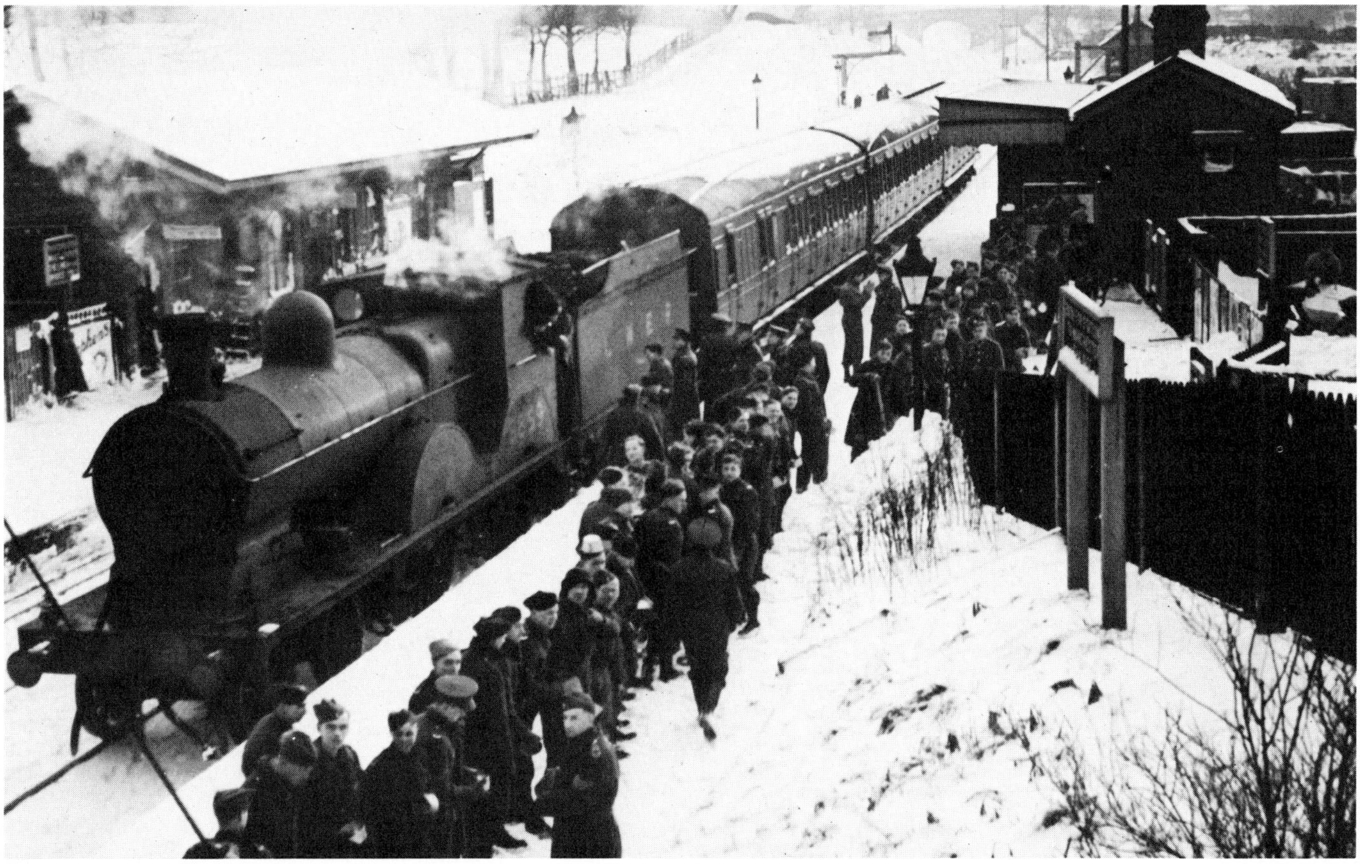

Rose Hill Marple was the northern most station on the Macclesfield Bollington and Marple Railway, which was promoted jointly by the Manchester Sheffield and Lincolnshire Railway and the North Staffordshire Railway in 1864. The station was opened on 2 August 1869. This view is looking towards Macclesfield in the winter of 1940 with a former GCR 4-4-0, D6 Class, 5859 at the head of a passenger train to Manchester. Presumably the troops have been on snow clearance duty. *Photograph: J M Ryan collection.*

Bosley Station c1910 looking towards Leek. Note the standard North Staffordshire Railway signal box and behind it the black and white crossing house and Station Master's house. Beyond the level crossing are the platforms and a substantial stone goods warehouse. Bosley Station was on the NSR Churnet Valley line from North Rode to Uttoxeter; it was opened on 13 July 1849 and closed on 7 November 1960. *Photograph: M Birchenough collection.*

A view of Congleton Station looking north c1905. The signal box on the left is the old style of NSR box, whilst the diamond-patterned brickwork on the station buildings on the right was a design feature that can still be seen on such station buildings as Etruria, Stoke, and Stone. The station was opened on 9 October 1848, on the section of the NSR main line from Stoke to Congleton. The original station buildings were demolished in 1965 as part of the electrification programme. *Photograph: B S Jeuda collection.*

This delightful view shows an open automobile approaching the level crossing at Congleton c1920; station buildings and signal box can be seen on the right hand side. *Photograph: B S Jeuda collection.*

Mow Cop Station c1900 looking south towards Stoke on Trent, taken from the staggered platform on the ''Macclesfield'' side. Note the level crossing gates and just to their left the unusual North Staffordshire Railway kissing gates. The station opened on 10 October 1848 and closed on 7 May 1962. *Photograph: B S Jeuda collection.*

Alsager Station was situated on the Crewe branch of the North Staffordshire Railway. This branch connected the Potteries with Crewe and was opened on 9 October 1848. This view c1905 looking towards Crewe shows the Station Master's house on the left and beyond the platform can just be seen a goods train and the goods warehouse; the station closed for goods traffic on 2 November 1964. *Photograph: B S Jeuda collection.*

The Sandbach branch of the North Staffordshire Railway linked the Potteries with the London North and Western Railway's line from Crewe to Manchester near Sandbach; it was opened on 21 January 1852. The main traffic on the line was limestone and coal for the Brunner Mond's works. This is a view of Wheelock Station c1905 looking south. It was opened on 3 July 1893 and closed on 28 July 1930. To the right is the Station Master's house and beyond the signal box can be seen the sidings into the Salt Union's Cheshire Works. *Photograph: J Minshull collection.*

Midland Railway 0-6-4T 2008 seen here at the newly built Cheadle Heath Station c1905. Under the New Mills and Heaton Mersey Railway Act of 1897, the Midland Railway took powers to build a "cut-off" line which reduced the distance to Manchester by 1½ miles. The station was opened on 1 October 1901 and closed on 2 January 1967. *Photograph: J M Ryan collection.*

A view of Heaton Mersey Station looking towards Stockport c1904 with a Midland Railway 0-6-0T locomotive at the head of a local passenger service to Manchester. The station building is to a standard Midland Railway design. Heaton Mersey Station, which opened on 1 January 1880 and closed for passengers on 3 July 1961, was part of a railway scheme called the Manchester South District Railway to serve the residential areas of South Manchester. This railway was taken over by the Midland Railway in 1877 and there was then developed a passenger service between Manchester Central and Stockport Tiviot Dale. *Photograph: J M Ryan collection.*

A view c1911 of the engineering works at Mirrlees Bickerton and Day, manufacturers of Diesel Oil Engines, near the Midland railway line at Bramhall Moor Lane, Hazel Grove. *Photograph: J M Ryan collection*.

The forecourt of Tiviot Dale Station, Stockport, which was also known as Teviot Dale Station c1904. Note the horses and cabs to the left and centre of the picture. This station, which opened on 1 December 1865, was part of the Stockport, Timperley and Altrincham Junction Railway which, with some other railways, was vested in the Cheshire Lines Committee on 5 July 1865; it closed entirely on 2 January 1967. *Photograph: J M Ryan collection*.

Another view of the forecourt of the Tiviot Dale Station, showing the Prince and Princess of Wales on a visit to Stockport on 7 July 1903. *Photograph: B S Jeuda collection*.

The viaduct at Reddish Vale carried the Great Central and Midland Joint Railway line from Stockport Tiviot Dale and from Marple towards Manchester. This section of line was opened during 1875. This photograph taken c1910 shows a Great Central Railway locomotive working an 8-coach passsenger train to Manchester. *Photograph: B S Jeuda collection*.

A pair of Midland Railway 4-4-0's at the head of the Royal Train on 12 July 1905 as it passes Bredbury Station and crosses the Bredbury viaduct which carries the Great Central and Midland Joint Railway over the Cheshire Lines railway from Stockport to Godley. *Photograph: J M Ryan collection.*

The Bredbury Colliery Company had sidings off the line at Bredbury. To the right of this 1905 photograph can be seen the sidings and the private owner wagons of the Colliery. *Photograph: J M Ryan collection.*

A view of Bredbury Station c1905 looking towards Marple with a complement of a dozen station staff. This station opened in December 1875. *Photograph: J M Ryan collection.*

A view of Romiley Station c1905 looking towards Bredbury. Note the signal gantry with three home signals, with the left signal covering the line to Stockport, the centre signal to Reddish, and the right signal to Hyde and Godley. *Photograph: J M Ryan collection.*

A view taken from Compstall looking south west with a train from Romiley crossing the Marple Viaduct, built in 1869, over the River Goyt. In the background, beyond the viaduct, is the Peak Forest canal aqueduct, itself built between 1802 and 1808. *Photograph: J M Ryan collection.*

Midland Railway 4-4-0 744 seen here at the head of a passenger train at Marple c1905. Marple Station was opened on 1 July 1865. Note the highly decorative awnings on both platforms. *Photograph: J M Ryan collection.*

The "cut-off" line from Chinley to Heaton Mersey necessitated major engineering works, one of which was the Disley Tunnel, 3,866 yards longs. Another significant engineering feature seen here c1905 is the viaduct at New Mills, over the River Goyt which separates Derbyshire from Cheshire. *Photograph: B S Jeuda collection.*

A view of Woodley Station c1905 looking south with the Cheshire Lines route veering off to the right towards Stockport Tiviot Dale with the line straight ahead going to Romiley and Marple. The station was opened on 5 August 1862 as part of a line from Hyde to Compstall promoted by the Manchester, Sheffield and Lincolnshire Railway. *Photograph: B S Jeuda collection.*

Apethorne signal box c1905, tall, imposing and built of stone, is situated at the junction of the Great Central and Midland Joint Railway line to Hyde (on the left) and the Cheshire Lines route to Godley (on the right). This box, of early Midland Railway design, dates back to c1880. *Photograph: J M Ryan collection.*

The Sheffield, Ashton-under-Lyne and Manchester Railway was the forerunner of the Manchester, Sheffield and Lincolnshire Railway, which in turn was the forerunner of the Great Central Railway. The SAMR built the line from Manchester to Sheffield, which was opened as far as Broadbottom Station on 10 December 1842, and finally extended to Sheffield on 22 December 1845. Here we see a GCR 4-4-0 1023 leaving Mottram and Broadbottom Station for Manchester c1908 at the head of a passenger train. *Photograph: J M Ryan collection.*

A view of Mottram and Broadbottom Station c1908 looking west towards Manchester. *Photograph: J M Ryan collection.*

A Great Central Railway 0-6-2T seen here leaving the west end of Woodhead tunnel, 3 miles 22 yards long, with a Sheffield to Manchester passenger train. The twin tunnel bores can be clearly seen, the one on the right opening on 22 December 1845 and the one on the left on 2 February 1852. The GCR water column is in the foreground. *Photograph: D A Kitching collection.*

A view of the former Manchester Corporation Waterworks Vale House reservoir at Longdendale looking east towards Woodhead. In the foreground can be seen the three foot gauge railway; first evidence of this railway was in 1868. It was electrified with overhead wire in 1904, but this was abandoned in 1949 and dismantled in 1954, being superceded by diesel haulage. The line closed for traffic in April 1968, with the last train running on 17 August 1968. *Photograph: J M Ryan collection*.

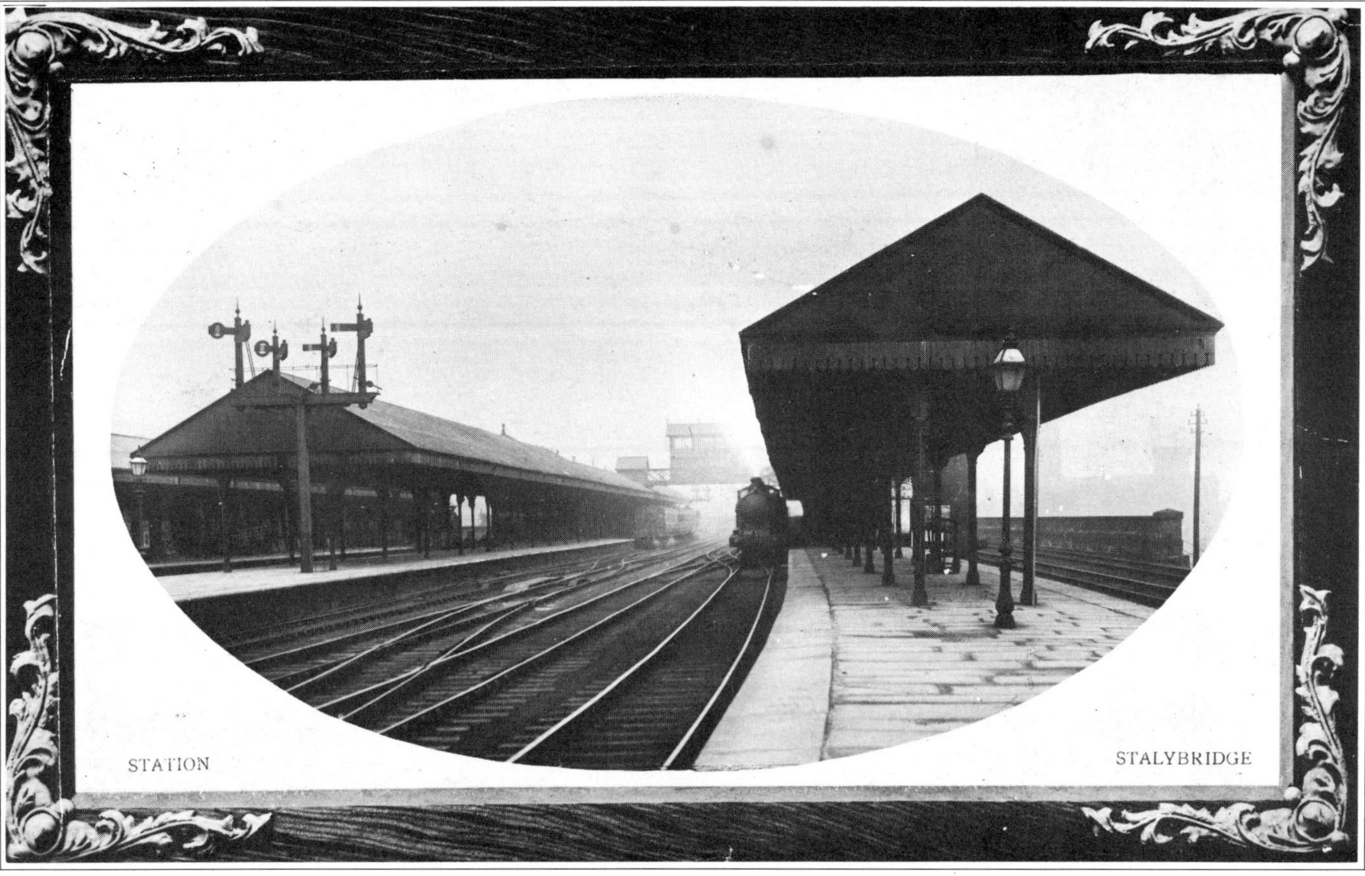

A view of Stalybridge Station c1908 looking east towards Yorkshire. The LNWR line from Stalybridge to Huddersfield was opened on 1 Augusut 1849. Note the signal box and gantry in the background which straddle the main line. *Photograph: B S Jeuda collection*.